Caspar Neher *Brecht's designer*

JOHN WILLETT

Caspar Neher *Brecht's designer*

Methuen . London and New York
in association with The Arts Council of Great Britain

Published on the occasion of the exhibition
organised by the Arts Council of Great Britain, 1986

Riverside Studios, London	15 January – 16 February
Cornerhouse, Manchester	26 February – 6 April
Graves Art Gallery, Sheffield	12 April – 18 May
City Museum & Art Gallery, Plymouth	31 May – 5 July

First published in 1986 in Great Britain
by Methuen London Ltd,
11 Fetter Lane, London EC4P 4EE
and in the United States of America
by Methuen Inc,
29 West 35th Street, New York, NY 10001
in association with
the Arts Council of Great Britain
105 Piccadilly, London W1V OAU

Copyright © John Willett 1986

Printed in Great Britain

ISBN 0 413 41240 7
ISBN 07287 0485 4 (Arts Council)

Exhibition organised by Roger Malbert
assisted by Lise Connellan

Exhibition designed by James Cumming,
Helen Powell and Ken Turner

Catalogue designed by Christopher Holgate

A list of Arts Council publications,
including all exhibition catalogues in print,
can be obtained from the Publications Officer,
Arts Council of Great Britain,
105 Piccadilly, London W1V OAU

Cover: 'Benares' by Caspar Neher for *The Rise and Fall of the City of Mahagonny* first
produced at Leipzig, 1930. Courtesy of the Austrian National Library, Vienna.

Caspar Neher, sitting for his portrait.
Photographed by his fellow-designer Hainer
Hill, who was then his assistant.

'Song of Mandelay', a drawing by Neher for
the song included in *Happy End* and quoted
in *Mahagonny*.

Contents

Brecht/Neher before and after the economic
crisis of 1929/30. *Above*: Projection sketch
'Activities of the Kilkoa menfolk at 7 a.m.'
for *Man equals man*.
Below: the Salvationist Joan Dark addresses a
Chicago meat-worker in *Saint Joan of the
Stockyards*.

Foreword

That an artist of such exceptional talent as Caspar Neher should be so little recognised, despite his association with some of the outstanding figures of twentieth-century theatre, is perhaps a reflection of the uneven distinctions of status attributed to the various arts in our culture. A stage designer's vision is contingent upon an author's, and therefore cannot claim to proceed from that position of absolute independence which the fine artist is assumed to enjoy; and it is linked to events which are ephemeral. Almost all of Neher's work occurred in collaboration with others, and the drawings were treated by the artist as a practical means of visualising action on the stage. They were afterwards discarded, sent to theatres or friends, not – to our knowledge – sold. Their intimate scale and Neher's own indifference to their value as works of art has allowed them to pass virtually unnoticed into history; there has been no exhibition of these drawings since shortly after Neher's death in 1962 and in the English-speaking world only a small number of opera designs has ever been shown.

The quality of the drawings is self-evident. What should perhaps be emphasised is the seminal influence they had on the development of Brecht's aesthetic. As John Willett shows, Caspar Neher was directly responsible for the visual aspect of many of the original conceptions of Brecht's plays. For this reason, and because Brecht is well-known to English-speaking audiences, we have chosen to concentrate on this side of Neher's career in the exhibition.

In accordance with what we imagine would have been the artist's own wishes, we have sought as far as possible to show the drawings not as isolated museum-pieces, but as working studies related to particular productions; by the use of projections, photographs and sound we have tried to suggest the ways in which Neher's ideas were ultimately realised on stage. The exhibition is being presented in centres where there is an active interest in the theatre in the hope that it will be seen by – and stimulate – the next generation of stage designers and directors.

The exhibition has been selected by John Willett from the main repositories of the artist's work. The contents of Neher's studio were left by him to the Theatre Collection of the Austrian National Library in Vienna, whose then Director, Dr Franz Hadamowsky, catalogued them. A considerable amount of further material is in the Cologne University's Theatre Museum at Schloss Wahn. Most of this was originally assembled by Neher's contemporary Carl Niessen, founder of the University's Collection. Neher was also closely associated with the Cologne theatres where his friend Oskar Fritz Schuh was Director of the Theatre and Opera from 1959 until the year of Neher's death. There are also several hundred drawings in the possession of the Brecht family in the Brecht Archiv in Berlin; this collection consists partly of designs made for Brecht's company, the Berliner Ensemble, between 1950 when the company was founded and 1957, and partly of drawings related to earlier collaborations and projects with Brecht dating back to the Munich production of *In the Jungle* in 1923. A number of drawings in Munich, where Neher first studied and worked, were acquired comparatively recently by the Theatre Museum there from various collections, notably that of Erich Engel, who worked closely with both Neher and Brecht. Augsburg, which was Neher's and Brecht's home town, has a small number of drawings in the Graphics Collection of the Schaezlerpalais. We wish to thank the directors of all these institutions and their staff for the loan of works and for the patience and generosity with which they have responded to our enquiries. Notably we are grateful to Dr Oskar Pausch, Dr Nitsch and Stefanie Winkelbauer of the Vienna National Library, Helmut Grosse in Cologne, Frau Barbara Brecht-Schall and the Brecht Estate in Berlin, Dr Eckehart Nölle and Dr Huesmann in Munich, and Dr Rolf Biedermann of the Graphics Collection in Augsburg.

The following have also given invaluable assistance: Dr J. Bellot of the Stadtbibliothek, Augsburg; Dr Oswald Bill of the Hessische Landesbibliothek, Darmstadt; Dorrette Boxberger of the Schauspielhaus, Zurich; Dr Rainer Budde of the Wallraf-Richartz Museum, Cologne; Dr Hans-Joachim Bunge, Berlin; Dr Anita Büttner of the Landesmuseum, Darmstadt; Peter Ebert; Hainer Hill; Dr Walter Huder of the Akademie der Künste in West Berlin; Hans Jaklitsch of the Archiv, Salzburger Festspiele; Martine Kahane of the Library of the Paris Opera; M. Boris Kochno; Georg Menzel, Cultural Attaché, Embassy of the GDR in London; Egon Monk; Jane Pritchard of the Ballet Rambert and Festival Ballet Archives, London; Larissa Rexroth of Universal Edition, Vienna; Eberhard Spiess, Deutsches Institut für Filmkunde, Frankfurt.

We are particularly grateful to Dr Frank Tornquist, Caspar Neher's brother-in-law, who represents the goodwill of the family and has taken a close interest in the project from its inception. Finally, our thanks are due above all to John Willett, who proposed the idea of the exhibition to the Arts Council, and whose unfailing enthusiasm, encyclopaedic knowledge and good humour have made it both possible and enjoyable to organise.

Joanna Drew   Roger Malbert
Director of Art   Exhibition Organiser

Baal. A big early drawing on a scroll which
used to hang in Brecht's room.

II

BERTOLT BRECHT *The friends*

The war separated
Me, the writer of plays, from my friend the stage designer.
The cities where we worked are no longer there.
When I walk through the cities that still are
At times I say: that blue piece of washing
My friend would have placed it better.

(About 1948)

Neher and his designs for Brecht

Caspar Neher never cared for the common German term 'Bühnenbild' (or 'stage picture') which he once characterised as 'a Nazi word'. 'The words "picture" and "stage"', he said, 'don't go together'. Nor did he like to be regarded as a 'Bühnenbildner', though he was frequently called one; since the very idea of such a person seemed like a hangover from the nineteenth century – not so bad as the stage painter or 'Bühnenmaler' perhaps, but still nevertheless a man who makes pictures. Admittedly this might perhaps be an acceptable approach to the designing of a ballet, which was where Diaghilev had so spectacularly brought in the 'pure' artist: first in the shape of the 'World of Art' painters of the 1900s, then with such Russian avant-gardists as Larionov and Goncharova and finally with Picasso, Derain and other great moderns centred on the School of Paris. But for the actors' theatre, with its need for an articulated stage and a modicum of illusion, the notion of 'stage pictures' was no more acceptable than the French term 'décor'. One of the first to realise this was Max Reinhardt, the greatest of pre-1914 Berlin directors, who after a brief moment of experiment with the work of such eminent painters as Munch and Corinth discovered in the versatile Ernst Stern a designer who took joyfully to the many technicalities of the theatre, from the cut of a costume to the jigsaw three-dimensional problems of the still new revolving stage. For particularly in Germany, with its advanced electrical industry, its dynasties of great theatre engineers or technical directors and its well-equipped theatres, the 'picture' approach was not enough.

Neher himself was in the first place an artist, as can be seen from his earliest drawings, but already there were artists who had gone beyond the provision of the 'Bühnenbild' to visualise the stage action and even the dialogue. So the artist–engraver Gordon Craig, who was by heredity an actor, became also a great, if frustrated director whose Moscow *Hamlet* still looks like a masterpiece; Adolphe Appia sketched settings for Wagner which might have allowed his operas to lead the theatre instead of holding its development back; Kokoschka wrote the visionary *Murderer, Hope of Womankind* which he expressed in brilliant drawings; Barlach published *The Dead Day*, whose primaeval figures were akin to his sculpture; Kandinsky created that largely wordless piece of Symbolist staging *The Yellow Sound*. Likewise Behrens, Van de Velde and other new architects became interested in the theatre, particularly around 1910, when there was a widespread move to break out of the limitations of the conventional theatre building, realised most effectively in Reinhardt's attempts at mass theatre in circus buildings and exhibition halls. And as the First World War approached all these elements started to come together in Expressionism, whose first plays were still waiting to be put on the stage.

In those days Casper Neher was an Augsburg teacher's son, a schoolboy who could draw and would occasionally jot down ideas for plays; and accident had it that he moved to the same secondary school and the same class as his junior (by one year) Bertolt Brecht. Already then these two struck up an artistic alliance, though it only became really productive in the course of the war, when Neher spent three grim years on the Western Front; one of its main features being that he applied his growing talent as a draughtsman to visualising some of his friend's first plays. At that point he was not a 'stage painter', nor yet a stage artist of any kind, but certainly he set out as an artist very sensitive to ideas for the theatre, and later when he came to make designs for it they were poetic visualisations rather than practical drawings or plans. Always this role of free poetic draughtsmanship in his work for the theatre created practical problems for him, even after he had mastered the techniques needed to see it realised; for his first impulse was to get the playwright's concept vividly and elegantly on to paper, and unless he himself or one of his trusted assistants was available to explain the details to the theatre involved he might find himself let down by its actual execution. He was a sporadic painter all his life, with moments when he longed to break away into painting proper. And yet intellectually he quite soon became what Brecht was to term a 'Bühnenbauer' or stage builder, whose concern was with materials and structure.

This was partly because he came to recognise from the mid-1920s onward that the theatre designer's major concern is to organise the static stage space for the progression of dramatic time and the movements of the actors. The flat canvas and its images or colours had to be secondary to the elements of three-dimensional space: sphere, cylinder, cube. Almost exclusively he saw the stage as a hollow box with a missing fourth wall; he was barely interested in the unconventional theatre spaces which fascinated Reinhardt, or the adaptable workshops and studios where so much exciting work is done today. But that hollow was made up of lesser hollows where the performer positioned himself or from which he moved, and it was the designer's job to single these out or play them down by his use of lighting, so as to help bring out the meaning of each scene. Particularly in the spoken play – as opposed to the more static and slower-moving opera – he should, in Neher's view, be guided by economy: walls and partitions no longer needed to be full height so long as they marked the playing area. Nor should the colours used be so bright as to distract from the author's words; moreover the different levels must be calculated in relation to the particular theatre, the intersection of sightlines determine the main positions. The colours, then, which he favoured were those of the traditional earth pigments – siennas, ochres, an Italian green, caput mortum, dull Venetian red – with only the most cautious use of anilin colours. The materials were natural ones: unstained wood, undyed calico or nessel. Furniture and props were restricted to those demanded by the action; they must not give evidence of the decorative touch of the 'stage painter' but rather of the usage which they have supposedly already undergone, which to the imaginative eye can suggest those unknown generations that used them before.

Once Neher's talents began to be known outside a narrow circle of friends in Augsburg and Munich, they were welcomed by the leading German (and in due course Austrian) theatres of the time; and after he had moved to Berlin in mid-1924 there were a number of outstanding theatre and opera directors with whom he repeatedly collaborated. They included Carl Ebert and the Dresden opera director Josef Gielen; Erich Engel who used him a lot in the 1920s and more fitfully later; Heinz Hilpert in the Nazi years; Walter Felsenstein both then and after 1945; Oskar Fritz Schuh from 1940 to the end of his life, for operas and plays alike. But first and foremost he continued (except in the Nazi years) to work with Brecht, and it was Brecht's special vision to which Neher's principles and preferences most closely corresponded. There is a poem of Brecht's dating from around 1932, just before the Nazi takeover, which he called 'Of all the works of man'. It expresses his love of old, much-used artefacts –

> The copper pots with their dents and flattened edges
> The knives and forks whose wooden handles
> Have been worn away by many hands . . .

– and of everything fragmentary, like those half-ruined buildings which suggest their complete form, yet 'have already served, indeed have already been overcome'; and it does so in terms that show how he must have welcomed Neher's mixture of exact, historically founded detail with economy of stage architecture. The same aesthetic of selective precision and implied human presence as we find in this and other poems (like 'The lovely fork' or 'The fishing-tackle', both written in California in the 1940s) is strongly expressed in the note of 1951 on Neher which can be found on pp. 70–72. Elegance, lightness, care: these are among the qualities which Brecht praises, and with them goes something that is right at the root of their collaboration: what he terms Neher's 'lovely mixture of his own handwriting with that of the playwright'.

*

For some five years after the end of the First World War Neher's experience of and work for the theatre was almost entirely bound up with that
of Brecht. He entered the Munich Academy to study illustration, but was
at first in some uncertainty as to what he really wanted to do. Brecht
broadly speaking was not. He had already written a play – *Baal*, which
Neher illustrated, calling it 'better than ten litres of schnaps' – and was
starting another, and he was counting on his friend for criticism and
collaboration. At home in Augsburg, it seems that Neher's parents were
not too glad that he was seeing so much of the young poet, who was
already much more radical politically than most of their group. Nonetheless he stood by Brecht in his personal crises; he went on expeditions to
the countryside with him; he joined him on the swingboats at the twice-
yearly fair (which figure in some of Brecht's early poems), and they discussed each other's work. 'He sets out his aesthetic', noted Neher early in
1919, 'and I disagree with him'. Two years later Brecht was trying to earn
money with film stories for a series of Bavarian cliff-hangers featuring a
detective called Stuart Webbs, and roped in Neher to help write them;
fortunately perhaps they got nowhere. Then he went off to Berlin for the
winter and finished writing his third play there: *In the Jungle*, whose
symbolist indications of colour (in this early version) accord well with the
drawings which Neher made of its characters, scratchily delineated in pen
over a damp wash. Looking back some thirty-odd years later the
playwright associated this transparently colourful play with the thin
sheets of paper on which he used to write it, walking up and down under
the autumn trees alongside the old city moat. 'Brown', goes the stage
direction for the first scene. 'Wet tobacco leaves. Soapy-green sliding
windows, steps. Low. Lots of paper'. The words Brecht chose, so he
recalled, were ones 'whose texture and colour were specifically designed
to make an impression on the senses'. Texture, colour, paper – the stuff
his father and uncle were helping to produce at the Haindl mills in
Augsburg – here is one bridge between the poet/playwright and the visual
world in which Neher was starting to move with such ease.

Following the bloody repression of the short-lived Munich Soviet in
the spring of 1919 the Bavarian capital was no longer a great progressive
centre of the arts: the city where famous 'foreigners' from other parts of
Germany, like Thomas Mann, Lion Feuchtwanger, Kandinsky and Rilke
had chosen to live. Even if it was not yet the 'Capital of the Movement',
as the Nazis called it after their failed coup of 1923, it was losing out to
Berlin as a place for the most promising artists; for it had vindictively
punished those who took part in the Soviet (like Ernst Toller and the
murdered anarchist Gustav Landauer), and its cultural organisation men,
in the State theatres and elsewhere, had developed cold feet. In this new

climate *Baal* was doubly rejected, both by the State theatre management and by the publishers who had been going to bring it out with Neher's illustrations. As a result the first of Brecht's plays to be performed was *Drums in the Night* in 1922. By now Neher had finally made up his mind to go into stage design, had been promised a job in the small but enterprising Munich Kammerspiele, and had made at least some drawings for this, actually the second of his friend's plays. But unfortunately the theatre had just engaged a new full-time designer to whom the director gave the job, and the eventual product was a classic Expressionist painted set which was neither very thoughtfully structured nor all that well suited to Brecht's ironic-poetic play. Instead, Neher had his theatrical initiation at the State Theatre in Berlin, where he went in the winter of 1922–23 to design what should, to judge from his drawings, have been a very beautiful production of Kleist's *Kätchen von Heilbronn* by Jürgen Fehling. The critics found it too pretty.

If Neher's most impressive work in Munich was for Brecht's adaptation of Marlowe's *Edward II* at the Kammerspiele, the immediately important one was the production of *In the Jungle* in the lovely eighteenth-century Residenz-Theater. For this brought together the combination of himself, Brecht and the director Erich Engel which was repeatedly to make such an impact on Berlin, first with the same play at Max Reinhardt's Deutsches Theater (with the bull-like young Fritz Kortner as the Chicago–Malayan timber merchant Shlink), then the *The Threepenny Opera* in 1928 and less favourably with its successor *Happy End*; finally in 1957 with *Galileo*, following Brecht's death. Of this trio Brecht was for a while prepared to play the provincial enfant terrible, making aggressive statements to the press, defending himself against accusations of plagiarism (which started with his Rimbaud references in *In the Jungle*) and advancing his earliest theories about the 'epic theatre'. Engel was always much more contained, and already was becoming known as a coolly detached director whose work was clean and logical: in some respects the answer to Berlin's surfeit of theatrical Expressionism. In *Coriolanus* at the beginning of 1925 he and Neher followed much the same new approach to the classics as had been seen in *Edward II*, with Brecht sitting in on rehearsals; yet he also showed himself able to deal competently with the modern 'well-made' plays of authors like Bernard Shaw, Jules Romains and Noel Coward such as the Reinhardt theatres were now putting on, and he got Neher to design them. So while Brecht buried himself in the rambling coils of his vast new play *Man equals man* (itself developed from a project which he had discussed with Neher back in Bavaria) Neher was making his mark also in the orthodox theatre, where his designs for Leopold Jessner's modern-dress

Hamlet of 1926 (with Kortner playing Hamlet) attracted particular attention.

❋

With the première of *Man equals man* at Darmstadt in September 1926 a new phase began for Neher. First and foremost perhaps, this was a play in which he became creatively involved in a fresh way, helping Brecht to visualise its production by his sketches of different episodes: most strikingly in the Berlin State Theatre production of 1931, which was one of the high points of all Brecht's work. Secondly, it was the play which led Brecht in the spring of 1927 to begin seriously collaborating with Kurt Weill, thus initiating a new concern with music theatre for both Neher and himself. And thirdly the Darmstadt theatre was directed by Ernst Legal, who became one of the top administrators of the Prussian State Theatres and after 1945 directed the State Opera in East Berlin, while his successor was the Reinhardt actor Carl Ebert, whose enthusiasm for Neher's work was to be crucial in bringing the latter into mainstream opera. This new phase thus had two ultimately contradictory aspects. On the one hand it led eventually to a certain operatic orthodoxy in Neher's work of the 1930s and early 40s, which was also encouraged by his first regular post in a typical subsidised German theatre-cum-opera establishment when he joined the Essen City Theatres as head of design in 1927. On the other however it opened up one of the most productive stages in his work with Brecht, since it also pointed to *Mahagonny* and *The Threepenny Opera*, and through them to the extreme 'Lehrstück' phase of 1929–32. It does seem that Neher must have realised which way he was heading in the later 1920s, even if he had at the same time gone to Essen partly in order to be free to head away from Brecht. Thus the composer Rudolf Wagner-Régeny, who first met him at Essen (and was later one of his closest friends) found him difficult to make contact with in his then role as a self-conscious individualist – 'a member of the avantgarde who had already helped Brecht bring a new dawn to our prejudice-ridden theatre' – while to Ebert's then administrator Rudolf Bing he appeared 'as left as could be'.

What Neher had contributed specifically was, first of all, the flimsy, half-height curtain for scene changes within an act, as seen in *Man equals man* and in some of the *Jungle* drawings, along with the visible light fittings and the accompanying wires. Then for the 'little' *Mahagonny* at the Baden-Baden music festival – first of the Brecht/Weill works – he made a boxing-ring stage of unpainted wood, outside which non-actors could stand informally, and accompanied each song with projections that combined written comments with satirical drawings. For the full *Rise and*

Man equals man at the Darmstadt
Landestheater 1926. Design for Widow
Begbick's canteen and its realisation. In each
case the bar is right and the artificial elephant
centre, but note the half-curtain and the
unrealised idea for a sliding roof.

Fall of the City of Mahagonny at the Leipzig Opera (and later at the Kurfürstendamm Theatre in Berlin) he supplied fresh projections, which had come to constitute an element on their own without which that work could not make its proper impact. For *The Threepenny Opera* he put the small orchestra on stage in front of an ornate organ and rigged up two screens overhead for the projection of the song titles and occasional sententious phrases by Brecht. From these particular innovations came a number of principles which Brecht incorporated in his theatrical theories, with which they clearly accorded: the 'separation of the elements', with words, music and images each telling the 'epic' story in its own way; the 'literarisation of the theatre' by use of inscriptions; the visibility of the scene changes and the sources of light. Some at least of them could also be seen in the more radical opera productions which Neher had now also begun designing: *Wozzeck* at Essen, *Macbeth* for Ebert at the Berlin Städtische Oper, a modern *Carmen* for Legal at the Kroll Opera, Milhaud's *Le Pauvre matelot* for Gustav Gründgens and Janáček's *From the House of the Dead* for Hans Curjel, again at the Kroll. Particularly at the last of these houses, which Otto Klemperer had made into a unique centre for modern opera and the modern reinterpretation of opera, the avantgarde concepts of Neher and (however uncongenial he might find opera) Brecht were starting to filter into operatic production.

This now almost classic epoch in the short life of the Weimar Republic came to an end with the economic crisis of 1929 and the Nazi Party's ensuing triumphs in elections at every level, from student bodies up to the Reichstag itself. Economy measures, such as halted the great modern housing schemes, were quickly followed by nationalist pressure for a cultural backlash and by a growing antisemitic agitation. Thus the Kroll Opera was closed as early as 1931, when the Prussian Assembly which had subsidised it decided that it could no longer do so. A year later the Prussian government itself was abolished by the new Chancellor Fritz von Papen, and with it the basis for Berlin's enlightened arts administration; it was one of Papen's aims to do away with 'art bolshevism', a favourite target of Nazi propaganda. Klemperer duly went into exile under Hitler's Third Reich, as did Curjel, along with Ebert and Bruno Walter from the Städtische Oper. By then however Neher could feel confident enough about his experience and prospects as an opera designer to believe that he could survive the break.

Whether he also felt that some respite from Brecht's demands and influence would be a good thing we do not know, but certainly Brecht was a ruthless exploiter of his friends (of both sexes) wherever the interests of his work were concerned. This in part was what had finally exasperated Kurt Weill and made the production of *Mahagonny* in Berlin in the winter of 1931 such a tense affair. Neher, who was its joint director with Brecht, was persuaded to take over the rehearsals, and went on from there to work closely with Weill on his next opera *Die Bürgschaft* (The Surety), a largely choral piece which developed a similar concept of 'epic opera', with Neher providing a severe libretto with Brechtian features (direct addressing of the audience, identification of riches with political power) but without Brecht's disruptive personality. Encouraged by Weill, he next started another libretto, this time for Wagner-Régeny, under the title *Der Günstling* (The Favourite), and certainly such ventures were evidence of his versatility and theatrical sense. At the same time Brecht, with a new musical collaborator in the shape of the equally radical Hanns Eisler, was involved with his revolutionary didactic play *The Mother*, based on Gorky's novel. Aufricht, the lessee of the Theater am Schiffbauerdamm who had produced most of the Brecht/Weill works including the latest version of *Mahagonny*, certainly hoped that this would divert Brecht's attention from the arguments with Weill. Neher however proved to be quite equally committed to the new work, for which he designed yet another new and simple, portable setting and conveyed his ideas in fine, largely monochrome drawings. The object here was not just aesthetic but also political: the production had to put across Communist ideas (most tellingly in the songs with Eisler), and must be playable in ill-equipped halls as well as theatres. Rather amazingly, this aim could be achieved, despite some police interference, only a year before Adolf Hitler became Chancellor.

    Such was the background to that pivotal but essentially minor work *The Seven Deadly Sins*, which had been commissioned by the wealthy English patron of Surrealism Edward James for a new Paris ballet company directed by Balanchine and Kochno and featuring James's wife the Viennese dancer Tilly Losch. Weill was to write the music, which he wanted to take the form of a sequence of Brecht songs sung by Lotte Lenya; Neher to provide the designs. What made the whole operation significant however was not so much the actual product as its timing, for it came within weeks of the Reichstag Fire, when both Weill and the non-Jewish Brecht had hurriedly left Germany (with Neher driving the Weills in his car). Superficially it represented a surprising return by all three partners to a style and a setting – the old imaginary America of *Mahagonny* and, before that, *In the Jungle* – which both Brecht and Weill had discarded; nor was Neher much inspired by it, to judge from the surviving drawings. Underneath, however, lurked a bitter artistic-political reality: the dissolution of a great theatrical partnership. For after meeting in Paris in April 1933 to complete the work, the three collaborators dispersed in different directions: directions which were to separate them for

a decade and a half, and in some respects for ever. Thus Neher returned
to a Germany whose new régime he did not like; nor in principle was it
much disposed to like him. Reputedly he had considered emigrating, but
was dissuaded by Weill. Weill himself remained for a time in Paris, producing a mixture of symphonic music and relatively trivial theatre work
(like his musical *A Kingdom for a Cow*, which was performed in
London), then moved to the United States in the mid-1930s to begin his
remarkable second career. Brecht went to Denmark, where he settled till
1938, then went to the States too, after short but productive stays in
Sweden and Finland and a trip across the USSR. Choosing to live within
reach of Hollywood, the great 'lie market', he was some 2,000 miles from
Weill, which may be one reason why their few attempts at collaboration
there never came to much. Neher, so far as we know, neither met nor
corresponded with Brecht till after the Second World War, when a fresh
phase of their collaboration began. He saw Weill a few times in 1934 and
1935 when travelling outside Germany, but if he ever thought of working
with him again the idea came to nothing when Weill died in 1950 without
having once returned to Europe.

✻

Within German culture as a whole, and again within the German-
language theatre (which also embraced Austria and Switzerland and the
German-speaking enclaves in Eastern Europe), the split was total. A very
few of the anti-Nazi exiles – mainly designers, composers and a small
number of particularly famous or versatile actors – managed to get
beyond the language barriers which now faced them, but writers like
Brecht were dependent on the dwindling number of German language
theatres still free from Nazi control. Conversely the well-subsidised
theatres within Nazi Germany (and, from 1938 on, Nazi Austria) were
dependent on the talents of such non-Nazis as Neher. He was by no
means alone in this new situation, for among those who had chosen to
remain were Engel, Wagner-Régeny, Falckenberg of the Munich Kammerspiele (who had given Neher and Brecht their first jobs), Gustav
Gründgens and Heinz Hilpert (both of whom had been hoping to stage
Saint Joan of the Stockyards before the nationalist reaction became too
severe), as well as Piscator's former designer Traugott Müller and the star
of the 1928 *Man equals man* Henrich George. Fortunately for Neher, as
the régime settled down these people moved into controlling positions:
notably Gründgens at the State Theatre – see the film *Mephisto* for a
critical view of his career as Goering's protégé there – and Hilpert at
Reinhardt's former theatres. But not only was the apparatus of cultural
control via Goebbels's new Chamber of Culture both powerful and rigid,

with a State Dramaturg to supervise the repertoire and a State Stage Designer to oversee errant artists like Neher, but the officially acceptable creative standard sank almost overnight to that of the former artist Hitler and the former writer Goebbels: that is to say, a mishmash of Wagner, the classic German drama, Dürer, Altdorfer and the nineteenth-century Munich genre painters. For National Socialist ideology dictated a nationalist, heroic-optimistic, morally elevating Nordic (i.e. non-Latin, non-Slav, above all, non-Jewish) art which would take its models and to a great extent its style from the period before 1900. The radical culture of the Weimar Republic was to be stamped out as negroid, semitic and decadent: hopelessly tarnished with the great national shame of the Versailles Treaty and the socialist 'stab in the back' of November 1918.

From inside Germany this system was just bearable if the artist knew how to operate it: to concentrate on the national cultural tradition, try to make use of its best aspects and work for those few organisations that seemed determined to maintain high standards within the limitations of the imposed ideology. Accordingly Neher, who at first appeared suspect to the authorities because of his association with Brecht and Weill, not only could continue to devise librettos (four in all) for Wagner-Régeny but found himself once again regularly in work from the beginning of 1934 on. This was primarily for the Frankfurt Opera, whose Intendant had useful political contacts, then later in Berlin at the Deutsches Theater from 1938 until its wartime closure in 1944. Here, under Hilpert, Neher seems to have made himself acceptable, for the Reich Dramaturg (a Nazi party journalist called Schlösser) wrote approvingly of his designs for *The Tempest* in Engel's production, contrasting it with the virtual 'cultural bolshevism' of Fehling's State Theatre production and Traugott Müller's sets. From outside the closed world of Fascism however such achievements looked rather different, while the self-evident fact about Neher's work in Vienna from spring 1938 on – first under Hilpert at the Theater in der Josefstadt, then from 1940 with Oskar Fritz Schuh at the opera – is that, for all their professional and personal merits, both his patrons owed their positions to Hitler's so-called 'Anschluss', or unopposed takeover of Austria (and its cultural institutions) in March 1938.

✻

The Reich capitulated to the Allies in May 1945. Brecht began planning his return to Europe during the course of 1946. If he felt any kind of resentment against Neher there is no evidence of it, and he may well have shared Fritz Kortner's view that his old friend 'never had any [convictions]. Not even in the Nazi period'. More important, probably, was the fact that he *was* a friend, and one whose contribution had always been

Start and finish of the fifteen-year gap.
Above, set for the Brecht-Weil, ballet *The
Seven Deadly Sins* (1933). Below, the
prologue to *Antigone* (1948) set in the ruins
of Berlin.

essential to Brecht's creations. Accordingly as soon as Brecht had found out where Neher had landed up – it turned out that he was then temporarily stuck in Hamburg – he wrote a quite short letter to say that 'the best thing would be if we could resume our collaboration in the theatre as soon as possible'. Though he hoped that Neher might be able to send designs for the Hollywood production of *Galileo* (which Brecht and Laughton were then preparing) in the event this proved impossible, so they arranged to meet in Switzerland, where the Zurich Schauspielhaus had kept the alternative German theatre alive right through the war – giving, among many other important productions, the premières of three of Brecht's big exile plays. Neher, who had already begun moving there, now joined Teo Otto, his former Kroll Opera colleague, as a staff designer for the Schauspielhaus for three years; Hilpert too was in Switzerland, which became a vital collecting point for the remains of the pre-Nazi theatre. For Neher this may well have been his first introduction to works like *Fear and Misery of the Third Reich* and *Mother Courage*, which had not of course been available in Nazi Germany or Austria but were well known to Otto, Wolfgang Langhoff and other of the Communist exiles in Zurich. And certainly his designs for them displayed a new freshness and freedom, even before Brecht himself arrived. Thus his *Fear and Misery* drawings are a bitter commentary on Nazism, while the *Courage* series display the mastery of period and detail which he had developed since 1933, while subordinating this to a marvellous sense of humour and life which almost goes beyond the play.

It was in this spirit that he got down to work with Brecht in the months following the latter's arrival, and from the outset it looked as it they were going to achieve great things – though it still had to be decided how and where. Having separated nearly fifteen years earlier following a relatively lightweight work, their first joint effort after the great divide was not only just as crucial for their working relationship as *The Seven Deadly Sins* had been, but also a small masterpiece in itself. For this was the Swiss *Antigone* production which only ran for a few performances but was unforgettably recorded in a long series of photographs commented by Brecht in classical hexameters. And from then on it appeared that the partnership – while in many ways different from before – had adapted to meet the developments in both men's work, and might turn out to be as productive as ever. Perhaps it was a pity that the many other jobs to which Neher had become committed prevented him from designing either the Zurich *Puntila* (fourth of Brecht's big plays to have its première at the Schauspielhaus) or the Berlin *Mother Courage* which convinced not only Germany but the rest of Europe that here was a new kind of theatre. But he agreed to join the Berliner Ensemble which Brecht and his wife Helene Weigel now set up in East Berlin to carry on from *Courage*'s success, and the work which he did for this new company, particularly on its opening production of *Puntila* and the two projects that followed, is visibly a development of their Swiss collaboration.

Both projects resulted in fine drawings, and it seemed that the composition of the company itself – a mix of anti-Nazi actors from Zurich (including the great Therese Giehse) with old agitprop hands from the Soviet emigration, cabaret artists from the west and unknown young Germans, along with Berthold Viertel among the directors and Eisler and Paul Dessau to write the music – was promisingly balanced. But one of the projects in question, Lenz's *The Tutor* which to Neher was an outstanding achievement, was only included in the repertoire at the last moment, while the other, Brecht's new play *The Days of the Commune* over which Neher took particular trouble, was cancelled on the insistence of the Socialist Unity (i.e. in effect Communist) party. That was at the beginning of 1950, and from then on matters got worse. The party aesthetes became critical, sometimes in terms reminiscent of the Chamber of Culture; Viertel went off to Vienna after one production; Wagner-Régeny's *Darmwäscher* (or *Persische Episode*) opera with its Neher libretto and three or four Brecht songs was held up; the *Mother Courage* film project ran into trouble; the Zurich actors began to drift away. In 1951 came the controversy over the anti-war opera *Lucullus* which Dessau had composed on the text of a 1939 radio play by Brecht, and for whose production by the State Opera Neher had designed the sets. More tellingly, perhaps, from his point of view, in 1952 the company performed a potboiling play by Nicholas Pogodin called *Kremlin Chimes* in which Lenin appeared 'ex machina' for all the world (commented Neher in his diary) like the emperor Franz Josef in *White Horse Inn*. With its old-style conventional sets by John Heartfield – then having to fight against accusations of 'Formalism' – this to Neher was 'the end of the Berliner Ensemble'. An undated request from Käthe Rülicke, one of Brecht's assistants, to write a few words on 'das realistische Bühnenbild' – literally 'the realistic stage picture', a phrase that the Reich Stage Designer too might have used – led him to the outburst quoted on pp. 75–77. Nor was he pleased to hear from his assistant Hainer Hill that Brecht was now damning all those members of the company who were not prepared to move house to East Berlin.

Already in 1951 Neher had taken another regular job in West Berlin as designer for the Schlosspark and Schiller theatres, while even before leaving Zurich he had become closely involved with Wagner-Régeny's fellow-composer Gottfried von Einem and Schuh from Vienna in the revival and modernisation of those Salzburg Festivals which Reinhardt had founded with Hugo von Hofmannsthal and run until 1938. This was not in the first place expected to replace Brecht's affairs in his priorities, for the original idea, as discussed with Von Einem in Zurich, had been that Brecht would become involved in the Festival, much as Hofmannsthal had been in Reinhardt's day, and it was hoped (even by Brecht too despite his commitments in Berlin) that he would be able to combine the different activities while mainly living and working in the East. Next came a plan for him to write a new Festival play to match Hofmannsthal's *Everyman*, whose performances outside the cathedral had been such a feature before Hitler.

By then Schuh and Neher together had started the operation by staging Von Einem's opera *Danton's Death*; a year later Neher, whose wife was Austrian, applied for and was given Austrian citizenship. Then in spring 1948 Von Einem suggested that it might help the still stateless Brecht's involvement if he were to do likewise; and after another twelve months he too formally applied. Whether or not this would have brought him effectively to Salzburg or led him to complete the promised *Dance of Death* for that city is a matter for speculation, but as it turned out the granting of citizenship to Brecht was made a matter of controversy by the anti-Communist Austrian press, and the result was to weaken his friends' position from 1951 onward. This was important to Neher, who had a high and justified regard for Schuh – probably the most rewarding and effective of his collaborators after Brecht – and he was to remain committed to the notion of a non-reactionary, open-minded, not too conspicuously moneyed Salzburg up to the end of the decade. But first of all Von Einem was removed from the Festival Committee, then the (advisory) Artistic Board of which he became chairman in 1954 (with Neher and Schuh among its members) was rendered ineffective; finally he was squeezed out altogether when, against their strongly expressed recommendations, Herbert von Karajan was made overall artistic director in the spring of 1956. In the course of this interesting intrigue Neher, it seems, was officially warned off further collaboration with Brecht by Egon Hilbert, the chief administrator of the Austrian national theatres under the Minister of Education. So we find Neher drafting a letter in autumn 1952 to tell Brecht that he had been forced to accept Hilbert's demand, since 'even to work in the East is now regarded as political activity' such as he had undertaken on oath not to indulge in. 'This is an appalling situation,' he concluded, 'but I am sure you will be able to understand it'. Appalling or not, it fitted Neher's own increasing disillusionment with Berlin as a whole, prompted particularly (it seems) by his disqualification for a professorship at the West Berlin Academy of Art. Ironically enough the two reasons which he was privately given for this were (i) that he collaborated with Brecht, and (ii) that he was an Austrian subject.

٭

Neher poses important problems, which range much further than do his life and work. For the division which split German culture into two mutually hostile halves during the central twelve years of his adult life not only foreshadowed that deeper division which has kept the two German states apart since 1945, but also in some measure resembled the split that runs right across Europe today. In such ways the life of a theatre artist, working in a collaborative business and very vulnerable to official intervention, is much more obviously symptomatic than that of the independent painter or sculptor. His style and the mood of his drawings vary, for he is engaged not only with his own feelings and judgement but also with the plays he works on, the directors and actors he works with and the audience who will see the result: thus a resourceful artist like Neher may swing from austere economical settings shaped exactly to the play, to ornate structures whose main point is to impress the spectator with their grandeur, maybe even the grandeur of the organisation putting on the performance. What then is the role of conservatism and innovation in such a man's work, and how far does the aesthetic contrast between the two areas correspond to the political one? Did the Nazis, for instance, have pragmatic reasons for their hatred of the radical art and theatre of the 1920s? Is there a political significance to the Communist – or more precisely Stalinist – suspicion of the artistic policies which Brecht pursued in the early days of the Berliner Ensemble, or more than accident in the GDR's then insistence on some of the very values that were insisted on under the Third Reich: the 'positive' hero, the nineteenth century realism, the sanctity of the national heritage? Again, how do we draw the line – both practically and aesthetically – between the backward-looking opera of the semi-musical rich and the new experimental opera that was developed by Weill and his like in the 1920s with the support of the Prussian arts administration and the heads of Universal-Edition? Do such genres still stand for what they stood for in Neher's difficult lifetime? How far do the practical aspects and the aesthetic in fact coincide? Is the supposedly rarefied world of the arts to be judged by different standards from the world of everyday? All these questions are implicit in the ups and downs of Neher's experience.

   Most clearly perhaps they emerge from first-hand observation of his work, and perhaps some of the answers then begin to emerge too. In the English-speaking countries unfortunately we have mainly seen its more traditionalist aspects, for with the exception of Schuh's visit to Sadler's

Wells in summer 1957 with his production of the Büchner (as opposed to
the Berg) *Woyzeck* Neher has appeared as an opera designer in collaboration with Carl Ebert and in the most expensive opera houses; and
however excellent his original designs there, they have sometimes been
the third or fourth repetition of some earlier version of the same work:
Wozzeck, Ballo in Maschera or *Macbeth.* Even where the Berliner Ensemble has been seen (which is only this side of the Atlantic and since
Brecht's death) his influence, though basic to its staging, has been felt at
second hand – as in their cut-down *Mahagonny* of the 1960s – since apart
from *Galileo* and the preliminary designs for *Coriolanus* with their slight,
perhaps deliberate echo of Albert Speer he made no direct contribution
after his undertaking to Hilbert and the Austrians. Yet right up to that
point his drawings for Brecht seem wonderfully alive and instructive, not
least because of the contrast between that life – which is like the life of
the Weimar theatre at its most vital – and his possibly worthier and more
dignified, probably much better paid drawings for conventional theatre or
opera establishments. Sometimes, we may infer, Neher found Brecht's
ideas and personality intensely inspiring: at others he (and, it seems, some
of his other friends) thought that he was being overborne by it and ought
to be doing the more traditional kind of design at which he became so
good. And true enough, Brecht was not in the normal sense a particularly
nice man, and the intensity of his focus on his own work could be difficult for those of comparable talents to put up with for long. It is however
immediately evident from any serious comparison of Neher's 'Brecht'
work with the rest of his graphic oeuvre that Brecht's influence was from
start to finish not merely stimulating but conducive to Neher's own particular genius. Brecht may have asked too much of his old friend; he may
have made life awkward for him (as he did over the ambiguities of his
intentions with regard to Salzburg). But he understood better than
anyone perhaps what Neher could do, and he could somehow communi-
cate the importance and the excitement of his doing it.

If this is what Brecht achieved for Neher's art, what then about
Neher's contribution to Brecht's? This is a fairly straightforward matter
of theatre history, for although Neher is often overlooked by seekers for
avant–garde or 'underground' theatre in the Germany of the 1920s his
innovations are clearly on record. The originality of his 'Bühnenbau' as
opposed to 'Bühnenbild' (or structural in lieu of pictorial) approach to
the stage is not confined to his work for Brecht, but it did correspond to
Brecht's own way of piecing together selected episodes in a story, and
this method (which has been termed 'selective realism') does seem the
most thoroughgoing stage application of the great avant–garde structural
principle of montage. The 'literarisation' of the theatre, as Brecht termed

Europe returns to life after World War Two.
In the *Ares's Chariot* revue project 'the
Goddess of Trade acquires an egg on the
black market'. In scene 9 of *Puntila* the
drunken landowner throws out his daughter's
fiancé.

Neher's use of projected inscriptions in *The Threepenny Opera*, gave the *monteur* (or fitter) an additional ingredient for his carefully chopped-up mixture; the 'separation of the elements' as seen in *Mahagonny* represented a new, similarly disjunctive method of overcoming the Wagnerian mushing together of sound (lovely), words (unintelligible) and setting (in those days for the most part dreadfully old-fashioned) in a so-called 'total work of art'. The sad thing here was that this separation was never practised quite as the three collaborators intended it, though it might prove startlingly effective even today.

Above all, however, Neher's contribution was a simpler and more fundamental one, because he could see the playwright's ideas in operation almost as soon as he had voiced them, then use his controlled sensitivity to line and colour to set them down in an alternative form as a supplement to the words of the script. This was likely to be of great value to the director's or the playwright's own need to visualise the grouping, atittudes and actions of the characters on stage; indeed when Brecht was working with Laughton in America on *Galileo* it was an aid that he particularly missed. But in the case of the earliest plays, and again with *Antigone* and the *Wagen des Ares* revue project following his postwar reunion with Neher it was almost as if the artist were writing the same play in his own medium. Easy as it may be for our own society to laugh now at the Old School Tie, an accident of schooling in pre-1914 Augsburg meant that Neher was in on the genesis of some of our century's outstanding achievements. It gave him a wonderful role that called repeatedly on all his energy and inspiration. In a time of terrible divisions and massive tragedies it brought him not only frequent exasperation but, to judge from the pictures, a lasting association with imagination and beauty, seriousness and fun.

BERTOLT BRECHT *About a painter*

Neher Cas rides across the sands of the desert on a
      dromedary and paints a green date palm in
      watercolours
(under heavy machine-gun fire).

It's war. The terrible sky is bluer than usual.

Many fall dead in the marsh-grass.
You can shoot brown men dead. In the evening you can
      paint them. They often have remarkable hands.

Neher Cas paints the pale sky above the Ganges in the
      morning wind.
Seven coolies prop up his canvas; fourteen coolies prop up
      Neher Cas, who has been drinking
because the sky is beautiful.

Neher Cas sleeps on the hard stones at night and curses
      because they are hard.
But that too he finds beautiful (the cursing included)
He would like to paint it.

Neher Cas paints the violet sky above Peshawar white
      because he's got no blue left in the tube.
Slowly the sun eats him up. His soul is transfigured.
Neher Cas painteth for evermore.

At sea between Ceylon and Port Said, on the inside of the
      old sailing ship's hull, he paints
his best picture, using three colours and the light from two
      portholes.
Then the ship sank, he got away. Cas is proud of the picture.
It was not for sale.

(About 1917)

CASPAR NEHER *Report on the Jungle*

Baal sat beneath a tree eating; grew fat and burst. After that
  he remained for a while seated.

As for Mannetou, he took the rib of a man and made a
  woman, that – incidentally – happened. Flying past, he
  touched Adam's index finger with his own.

In September, again on a Sunday, Shlink bought a soutane
  and it occurred to him to act himself. That was the
  start of the evil business. How else would Shlink ever
  have become known? He fell in love with a youth
  called Garga, George, and loved him unto his death.

But one day Garga threw off his coat and began acting
  Garga, and that was fatal. Once they even got each
  other mixed up; and the realisation caused the death of
  one of them. His death might have come about even
  without this realisation; in any case the thought
  occupied him for quite some time before he died.

The play has nothing to do with any racial dispute. It is
  probably a mere accident that the Eastern race should
  perhaps be older than the Western. All human
  individuals however have the same number of red cor-
  puscles. From this arises the algebraic hypothesis that
  $a = a$; therefore Shlink = Garga and Garga is
  equivalent to Shlink.

Undoubtedly however Mannetou hovers over them all,
  cloaked in his thick soutane (with a dirty, rather
  yellow cloud), enthroned above the waters – for now
  he has grown indifferent to the chaos – he is much
  concerned with himself.

The treetops of the jungle shut by mutual agreement, and the
  sky has become an independent affair or none at all.

Baal however, in the days when he was still seated beneath
  the trees, could see clearly how the tree's branches
  divided up that rather yellow cloud.

CASPAR NEHER *From the libretto for Kurt Weill's opera 'Die Bürgschaft' – start of Act 3*

Man does not change,
it is the conditions that alter.
Likewise the system creating the conditions
alters up to the day
when it perishes by its own alterations.

The railway line was completed,
daily the trains brought new people into the land.
The cities grew,
and many waited for the better times
which they had been promised.

Just a few made money.
They had recognised
that the world is governed by laws,
that the laws are created by power
and the power by money.

So the poor separated from the rich.
But the number of the poor was greater
than that of the rich.
And the rich said to the poor:
What governs the world
is laws.

And they failed to tell them
that the laws are created by power
and the power by money.
So they came to the four gates
through which all would have to go,
the four gates that are called
War, Inflation, Hunger and Illness.
And through those gates
they all must go.

In the sixth year
since the Commissioner's arrival
war broke out
on that land's frontiers
and there was war.

Night and day
the army marches
over fields and meadows
with tanks and guns
and the dust eats up the miserable song
from parched throats.
So they march
deeper and ever deeper
into the crater
from which none comes back –
not one mother's son.

(c. 1932)

Neher's set for *Die Bürgschaft* by Kurt Weill,
for which he wrote the libretto. First staged
by Carl Ebert at the Städtische Oper, Berlin
in 1932.

BERTOLT BRECHT *'The Oil Song' from Neher's libretto for 'Der Darmwäscher'*

Lovely is the velvet perfume of the roses
In cottage gardens
And the precious smell of sesame
But they're nothing if you compare them to the smell
Of oil.

As for the smells of fresh-baked bread
And of peaches and pistachio trees, they too
Are good, but they can't ever match the smell
Of oil.

Even the smell of stallions and of
Camels and of water-buffalos
Delights the expert
But the one smell you can't resist comes
From oil

(1951)

Costume design for Engel's production of
Coriolanus 1925.

The designs for Brecht *and some ramifications*

Costume design, 'George Garga' for Brecht's
In the Jungle, 1923/4.

The designs for Brecht and some ramifications

I. The Munich Years

Before moving to Berlin in autumn 1924 Neher was more a poet in watercolour than a skilled stage designer. Extremely close to Brecht's ideas, he as yet had virtually no experience of the work of any other playwright. His acquaintance with the Elizabethan dramatists, which was to be important throughout his life, seems to have been made with and through Brecht; they visited the Munich theatres together, and even the characteristic colours which he began using – the dull reds and earth browns – seem to link up with their joint visit to southern Italy that summer.

1: Baal. Neher's earliest drawings for this first play are in the nature of illustrations or visualisations of his friend's script, which was based dramaturgically on Büchner and thematically on Verlaine and Rimbaud. Some were intended for publication. Others are more theatrical, but seem like free attempts to match Brecht's imagination rather than actual stage designs. The imagery (like that of the play) is romantic without being Expressionist; the figure of Baal the poet brooding and loutish rather than conventionally poetic. The pen and watercolour technique used by the artist is reminiscent of that adopted by Klee in the war years or Grosz a little later: splintery line, delicate colours, wet washes.

Anxious to avoid controversy, the Munich theatres rejected the play, and as a result the first production (Leipzig, 1923) was not designed by Neher. Brecht laid little store by it. Then for the Berlin production of 1926, a single matinee performance co-directed by himself, he radically rewrote the play, which he now set in the rising technological society of the prewar years. Neher has left us some rather bigger drawings for an economic setting with naively painted flats, and characters in everyday dress. Photographs show its effectiveness. Oskar Homolka, a solid Slavonic type, played the poet.

2: Drums in the Night. The writing of this play, in the aftermath of the doomed Spartacist Rising in Berlin, coincided with Neher's discharge from the army and initiation as an art student in Munich. He discussed it with Brecht as he was revising it, and made some small exploratory designs. When the Munich Kammerspiele accepted it for production in 1922 Brecht hoped that they would let Neher realise his ideas. However, Otto Falckenberg the director preferred to give the job to the newly

Neher's unused design for Act 5 ('Wooden
bridge') of *Drums in the Night*. This was not
used for the 1922 Munich première, *(above)*
which was designed by Otto Reigbert.

appointed staff designer Otto Reigbert, who painted angular, Expression-
istic scenes slightly out of key with Brecht's ironic treatment of the
characters and his manic-defeatist returned soldier hero. Falckenberg's
Berlin production later in the year was also Expressionist. First of
Brecht's plays to be produced, *Drums in the Night* made his name
throughout Germany.

3: Jungle (later *In the Jungle of Cities*). This exotic play of 'incomprehen-
sible' conflict, based on a mixture of images from Rimbaud, Gauguin,
Kipling and the Chicago of Upton Sinclair, was started in Augsburg during the autumn of 1921 and completed that winter in Berlin. Brecht sent
it to Neher, who visualised his characters for him – the shiftless Garga
family, the Malayan entrepreneur Shlink, the underworld figures Baboon
and Worm – much as he had done with *Baal* and using a similar technique. This time however he was able to design the first production in
Munich (by Erich Engel, a director who became a lifelong colleague) in
the spring of 1923. Engel thereafter moved to Max Reinhardt's theatres in
Berlin, and was joined there a year later by Neher and Brecht. Together
they made their effective début with a second production of the play, in
which the powerful young Fritz Kortner played Shlink. Among the mass
of drawings which Neher made, it is not easy to distinguish between the
two productions, though there is evidence sometimes of the half-height
curtain which became typical of Brecht and may already have been
envisaged for the second production.

Both times the play was characterised by an almost Symbolist use of
colour and dusty, atmospheric lighting, which appear to have been built
into it from the first, when Brecht walked under the autumnal trees writing – on 'quite small thin sheets of paper' – the scene headed 'Green
papered attic'. Some at least of these headings were actually contributed
by Neher. After the Berlin production Brecht revised it to make the more
'neusachlich' *In the Jungle of Cities* as we now have it. Carl Ebert put
this on at Darmstadt in 1926, but without Neher's involvement.

II. The Elizabethan Experience
By the time of the first *Jungle* production both Neher and Brecht were
on the payroll of the Munich Kammerspiele, where their first joint
project was to be a production of *Macbeth*. This hardly got beyond preliminary discussions and a few drawings before Brecht decided, with his
mentor the novelist Lion Feuchtwanger, to adapt and stage Marlowe's
Edward II instead. Then in Berlin following the *Jungle* production both
men were involved with Engel in the staging of *Coriolanus*, once again

with Kortner in the lead; critics linked this with the Munich Marlowe. All three plays were crucial in Neher's development, and he, Brecht and Engel were more than once drawn back to them or (in Neher's case) to the equivalent Verdi operas. The experience is reflected also in Brecht's theoretical writings, where Shakespeare and the staging of Shakespeare are fundamental.

4: Life of Edward II (after Marlowe). Brecht began work with Feuchtwanger in the summer of 1923. He was to be sole director, Neher the designer and at the same time illustrator of the published text (Kiepenheuer, 1924). Again a very large number of drawings resulted, this time more clearly related to the stage (e.g. in some cases by sketch plans). They are still very small, but show a marked change in dominant colours, with much use of red-browns, bistre and pink. The many scenes – Parliament, the London streets, the battlefield of Killingworth, the camp near Harwich, the granary where Edward is taken prisoner, Shrewsbury Castle, the sewer in the Tower of London and so on – have a sinister, rather earthy beauty which seems borne out by the production photographs. The stage is uncluttered, the costumes of rough, rather stiff material, the make-up (e.g. the white-faced soldiers) exaggerated without being grotesque. All this looks forward to the *Antigone* production of 1948.

5: Macbeth by Shakespeare. One or two drawings, marked by Neher 'discussed with B. Brecht', relate to this project of 1922–23. There are also unidentified drawings by him which, like them, while clearly not intended for *Edward II*, are stylistically similar to those done for it.
   More than once in his writings on the theatre Brecht praises Neher's interpretation of the play, which he himself was to adapt for radio in 1927 but never again attempted to stage. Possibly however he was referring to the sets which his friend designed for Carl Ebert's production of the Verdi opera at the Berlin Städtische Oper in 1931, which seem closer to the poverty-stricken Scottish baronial castle described by him. These became classic, in that Ebert summoned Neher more than once to recreate them: at Glyndbourne in 1938 for instance and the Metropolitan Opera in New York in 1958–59.

6: Coriolanus by Shakespeare. Engel directed this with Reinhardt's actors, augmented by Kortner in the title part, in the Lessing-Theater, Berlin, at the beginning of 1925. Brecht, then one of Reinhardt's junior directors, was involved in the rehearsals. Neher's designs – for the Senate, the Forum, the battle scenes and so on – are akin in style and spirit to those for *Edward II* and the *Macbeth* project.

In 1937, by leave of Goebbels's Propaganda Ministry, he and Engel returned to the same play, which they staged for Reinhardt's Nazi-appointed successor Heinz Hilpert. The comparative monumentality of Neher's designs, and their lack of life, vividly illustrate the destructive impact of Nazi ideology even on so individual an artist. Finally in the winter of 1951–52, once settled back in Berlin from exile, Brecht started translating and adapting the play with a view to producing it with his own East German company, and Neher made some preliminary designs. The project bogged down, but five years after Brecht's death the company revived it and asked whether Neher wished to carry on. Now an ill man, he left the job to his successor Karl von Appen.

III. 'Neue Sachlichkeit' and republican Berlin

From 1927 to 1930 Neher was closely involved in Brecht's partnership with Kurt Weill, which itself arose out of the transitional work *Man equals man* and the mock-American 'Mahagonny Songs' in Brecht's first book of poems. At the same time he was running his own design department for the city theatres in Essen, a task which broadened his experience and helped to interest him seriously in the staging of opera. This new phase began with the first version of the Brecht/Weill *Mahagonny* opera, the co-called 'Songspiel' performed at Hindemith's 1927 music festival, and Neher shared in all the further developments of that work – of which his projections came to form an integral part. He also contributed to the spectacular success of their *Threepenny Opera* and thereby became part of the team at E. J. Aufricht's Theater am Schiffbauerdamm, whose management underwrote it. So long as the money lasted the group could also produce such works as *Happy End, Pioniere in Ingolstadt* (by Brecht's protégée Marieluise Fleisser) and a reduced version of the full *Mahagonny*. Brecht himself however began losing interest in 1929, when the political and economic crisis turned his mind elsewhere.

7: Man equals man. (Sometimes referred to by Neher as 'The four soldiers from Kankerdan'). Before coming to Berlin Neher had already been in on the conception of this play, which started as a tale of personality change in a Bavarian setting. There are some of his hundreds of unidentified drawings which might relate to it, whether at this early stage or in its Kiplingesque reincarnation of 1925, when Brecht and Elisabeth Hauptmann shifted the basic idea to British India. Three key productions followed, each designed by Neher. In 1926 Ebert did the play at Darmstadt, using the Brechtian half-curtain running on visible wires. Early in 1928 Engel staged it for the Berlin Volksbühne (these could be the

For Shakespeare's *Coriolanus*. Three different
visions and styles of drawing: left, before and
during the Third Reich; opposite page, after
its fall.

designs which Neher re-used for Essen in 1929). Then at the beginning of 1931 Brecht himself directed it for a handful of performances at the Berlin Staatstheater: a production which Sergei Tretiakov saw and compared to Meyerhold's constructivist *The Magnificent Cuckold* of 1922 with Popova's sets.

Neher left drawings for all of these. From the start he seems to have been inspired by the tin-hatted soldiery and the oriental setting, but in the case of the third he was prodigal with projections and production sketches showing episodes with snatches of dialogue floating in the air between larger-than-lifesize soldiers in sun helmets. Galy Gay, their victim and involuntary recruit, appears as a pear-shaped innocent, dressed apparently in pyjamas. Photographs and a clip of 9 mm film shot by Carl Koch show how these visions were realised: the flimsy wood and cloth setting under a few dangling lamps, in which Peter Lorre and Helene Weigel appear dwarfed by distorted soldiers with stuffed-out shoulders and/or stilts.

8: Mahagonny, later *Rise and Fall of the City of Mahagonny*. With Kurt Weill. Though this work is located in a fantastic Florida (with hurricanes, gambling and a desert) rather than India, there are cross-connections with *Man equals man*, whose third version was incidentally composed by Weill. The 1927 production ('Songspiel' version) was directed by Brecht on a boxing-ring stage backed by big Neher projections, which led him to formulate his theory of the 'separation of the elements' whereby the designer should make his own independent contribution, providing his own version of the story. This principle was implemented by Neher at the Leipzig première of the full opera in March 1930 and ensuing productions at Frankfurt and Kassel, followed in late 1931 by the lighter and less conventionally operatic production financed by Aufricht in Berlin. This last had Brecht and Neher as joint directors, but in the end Neher largely took over. Having already collaborated with Weill on some notes on the staging, he now went on to write the libretto of *Die Bürgschaft*, the composer's next opera.

The problem with this multiple involvement is that it is difficult to allocate Neher's surviving designs among the different productions. Many are for projections: the 'sharks' (arrival of the girls), 'the city of nets' (or 'Suckerville' in Auden's translation), Benares, money, love ('the crane duet'), greed, boozing, the eventual (prophetic) bombing of the city by low-flying planes. They show Neher's potentialities as a satirical draughtsman.

9: Unknown revue. Drawings somewhat in the *Mahagonny – Man equals*

Projections as an 'element' of opera. The set
for *Rise and Fall of the City of Mahagonny*
(?1930/31), with a projection for the last
scene.

1928. *Above*: execution of Galy Gay from the Volksbühne's *Man equals man*. *Below*: drawing for the last scene of *The Threepenny Opera*. Both directed by Erich Engel.

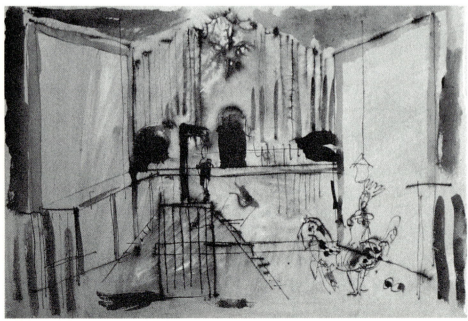

Man spirit may relate to a Brecht scheme of 1926 for a revue satirising 'Amerikanismus' or, more probably, to an idea for a 'Revue for the Ruhr' at the end of the 1920s, when Hannes Küpper was dramaturg at Essen (the chief Ruhr city) and Neher and Hein Heckroth the designers there.

10: The Threepenny Opera. This work was put together in such a hurry at Aufricht's instigation that Neher can hardly have done anything about it before the 1928 summer holidays. His drawings seem to reflect the ensuing confusion, since they are generally uneven and no very coherent group of them has survived. Some were supposedly for projections, though stage photographs and Brecht's notes suggest that for the first production the two screens either side of the stage were intended for song titles, initially designed by Neher, with the actual titles in his handwriting and an appropriate drawing: e.g. the delicate pen-and-watercolour sketch of bowler-hatted men relaxing, entitled 'Das angenehme Leben' (or pleasant living). (In production these were replaced by lettering only, evidently in another hand.) Some are brush drawings in Chinese white on a black ground. The beggars and their organisation are among the subjects (the whole thing deriving from Elisabeth Hauptmann's translation of *The Beggar's Opera*). Prostitution also figures.

Subsequently Neher was often asked to design other productions, including that in New York in 1933. Other notable versions were those at Munich (with new verses by Brecht) in 1949 and at the Royal Court Theatre in London in winter 1955–56. For G. W. Pabst's film version of 1930–31 – the one still shown in specialist cinemas – he designed only the costumes, of which we have rather sketchy brush drawings.

11: Happy End, its Runyonesque successor exactly a year later, was an equally confused if less inspired attempt to repeat the recipe, using the same collaborators. Brecht lost interest and later disowned the work in favour of 'Dorothy Lane' (i.e. Elisabeth Hauptmann, with whom the 'book' had once again started). There are however some fine pen and wash or gouache drawings by Neher, showing Hallelujah Lilian and other Chicago characters, while Brecht and Weill wrote 'Hosanna Rockefeller', 'Bill's Ballhaus in Bilbao', 'Surabaya Johnny' and other famous songs. Thereafter some of the material went into the making of *Saint Joan of the Stockyards* (14). There were no more productions till the 1950s.

12: Pioniere in Ingolstadt (or Manoeuvres in Ingolstadt, a smallish Bavarian town) was the young Marieluise Fleisser's second play. Brecht and Jacob Geis directed it with another fine cast at the same theatre while

Happy End (1929). *Above*: design for the
Salvation Army hall. *Below*: design for
backdrop.

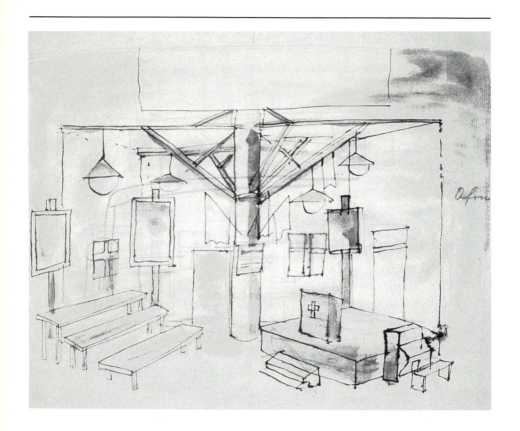

Also at the Theater am Schiffbauerdamm:
Manoeuvres in Ingolstadt by Marieluise
Fleisser (1929), co-directed by Brecht. Design
and stage photo.

The Threepenny Opera transferred for the second half of its long run.
Those few drawings which can still be located show a quite fresh
approach on Neher's part. They are relatively large, emphasising the blue
uniforms and red military faces, which are picked out in gouache. He
seems to be using knowledge acquired during the First World War, when
he made some well-observed sketches of his fellow-soldiers.

13: The Breadshop is an unfinished play about the economic depression,
somewhat akin to *Saint Joan of the Stockyards*. Neher made a few drawings using pen, wash and a touch of colour. The play was 'finished' post-
humously by Brecht's younger collaborators, and has been produced a
number of times.

IV. Marxism and the end of the Weimar theatre

Brecht lined up with the German Communist Party in 1929 at a time
when he was starting to explore the didactic possibilities of the Japanese
Nô drama and the new musical 'Lehrstück' that formed the subject of
Hindemith's festival that year. With a new collaborator, the composer
Hanns Eisler, he began trying to bypass the established or 'bourgeois'
theatres in order to find a politically committed, if possible working-class
audience. Neher, while siding with Weill over their 1931 *Mahagonny* production, nevertheless collaborated in the didactic, openly revolutionary
The Mother which Brecht and Eisler had derived from Gorky's novel.
Compared with this his work on *Saint Joan of the Stockyards* was less
radical, since for one thing the latter was intended for the conventional
theatre, while for another it could anyway not get accepted for production in the prevailing climate. Unrelated to his theatre work there were
drawings, now known only from photographs, which suggest that Neher
may around this time have been further to the left than is often thought.
    After meeting in Paris however, in the May following Hitler's accession
to power, the partners went different ways. This meeting of Neher,
Brecht and Weill took place in order to write and stage that unique ballet
Anna-Anna or the Seven Deadly Sins, a work in a mode which they had
already exhausted. Since two of them were now unable to work in Germany the commission was a godsend, and there seem to have been no
notable disagreements.

14: Saint Joan of the Stockyards. Neher left about half a dozen pre-Nazi
drawings for this play, which was Brecht's first major non-musical work
since the première of *Man equals Man* in 1926. One of them is a cover

Brecht's *The Breadshop*, an unfinished play about Berlin during the world economic crisis of 1929–33. *Above*: Chorus of unemployed workers. *Below*: Selling firewood.

design for its publication in 1932, and it is not known if the others were made with a specific production in mind. Among the possibilities – none of them realised – were one in Vienna which Viertel hoped to direct that year with Neher's namesake Carola in the lead, and another which Hilpert wanted to stage at the Deutsches Theater in the fateful year 1933. All that is clear from these sombre drawings of the slaughterhouses of Chicago, its unemployed and its socially engaged Salvationists, is that the play gripped the artist's imagination. Nearly a quarter of a century later he designed its première at Hamburg with Brecht's elder daughter Hanne Hiob as Joan.

15: The Mother after Gorki. The 1932 production was a remarkable achievement at a time when the Left theatre was suffering badly under economic cuts and the new timidity of the managements, who had been impressed by the organised reaction. Though it started in a theatre founded by Aufricht it was intended to be playable in halls and at political meetings, and as a result the set was minimal. The almost monochrome drawings show a playing area defined by canvas screens stretched between wooden posts. At the back is a bigger screen for projections – apparently photographic – and each time there is an imaginative grouping of the characters. There are also stage photographs which show that in the event the posts were made of gas-piping which acted as a frame for the canvas. The impression is simple and serious, in harmony with the text and with Eisler's music.

In 1951 Neher provided more colourful and more detailedly naturalistic designs for Brecht's production with the Berliner Ensemble. There were also rather clumsy projections by Heartfield and his brother.

16: The Seven Deadly Sins. Brecht's contribution to this Balanchine/Kochno ballet was the song texts and the story; later he added the phrase 'of the Petty Bourgeois' to the title. Weill wrote the music. Neher's drawings – by no means among his best work – suggest that he provided mainly designs for the costumes, along with seven hanging banners specifying the Sins, and some possible projections.

V. Hitler's Third Reich – a twelve year interval

Between spring 1933 and the end of the Second World War there is no evidence that Neher and Brecht ever met or corresponded. In the 1937 edition of his plays Brecht refers to his collaborator on *Mahagonny* and *Man equals Man* as 'R. Kass'.

The Mother, after Gorky. Neher's design for scene 2 – printing of the illegal leaflet – in the 1932 production, compared with his set for the Berliner Ensemble production of 1951.

Fear and Misery of the Third Reich.
Projections for the Basel production of
January 1947. Start ('The German March-
past') and finish ('Any protection against
gas?') of the sequence of scenes.

VI. Zurich – reunion, renewal and results

Arriving in Switzerland a year or more before Brecht got there from America, Neher designed both *Mother Courage* and *Fear and Misery of the Third Reich* without being able to discuss either play with his friend. This makes his drawings for them of particular interest, since they show his spontaneous reaction to the works in question – as also to the ending of the Reich itself. Then came the renewed collaboration as first seen in the Chur *Antigone*: a very important work for them both, whose power and beauty can be judged from Brecht's subsequent descriptions and the photographs taken by Ruth Berlau. There was also a new but unrealised project for a revue satirising various aspects of the late war – *Der Wagen des Ares* (or Ares's chariot) – whose surviving designs make one lament that it was not carried further.

17: Fear and Misery of the Third Reich. The projections which Neher designed for some twenty of the separate short scenes that make up this work constitute his most direct statement on the Nazi era. They are more or less monochrome pen and wash drawings recalling, as do the structure and spirit of this exceptional play, the *Disasters of the War* by Goya. Each was meant to accompany one stanza of the long poem with which Brecht linked the scenes, starting with a longer prologue termed 'The German March-past', here illustrated by an endless crowd – of refugees? emigrants? – anyway of ordinary people getting away from some great disaster. It harks back to the predictions of *Mahagonny* and to another uncaptioned drawing of around 1930.

In the Basel production by Ernst Ginsberg (one of the exiled actors in Zurich) the scenes were played on a plain red platform. The play had originally been designed for exile groups to perform before the Second World War, though there was also a wartime version called *The Private Life of the Master Race* which was performed in the United States.

18: Mother Courage and her Children. In 1946 the Zurich Schauspielhaus, who had given the first performances of this anti-war play in 1941 in a sombre setting by Teo Otto, revived it under the original director, Leopold Lindtberg, but with new designs by Neher. What Brecht thought of these when he arrived the following year we do not know; he almost certainly never saw the production itself. But the impression given by the drawings is one of extraordinary gaiety, and Neher carried this over into the designs which he made in 1949 for the proposed East German film version. Both sets of drawings remained for the greater part with Brecht, who had wanted Neher also to design the epoch-making Berlin production with Helene Weigel in winter 1948–49.

Two scenes for the second (1946) Zurich
production of *Mother Courage. Above*: scene
6: the funeral of Marshal Tilly. *Below*: scene
3: Military camp.

In the event however he used Otto's ideas reworked for the Deutsches Theater's stage and realised by Heinrich Kilger. The impression was overwhelmingly grey, despite the exceptionally brilliant lighting. It is fascinating to think how it would have turned out if Neher had done the job.

19: Antigone by Sophocles. In effect this joint production at the small town of Chur was a try-out of Brecht's and Neher's ideas and of their ability still to work together. It was also a test run for Weigel after years away from acting. The resources used were simple, and were vividly described by Brecht in his *Antigonemodell*, which also prints many of Ruth Berlau's photographs. Again Neher made many drawings of which the bulk remained with Brecht, but they are utterly unlike those for *Courage* – being large, simple and severe. Among them are one or two painted on silk with watercolour washes and touches of Venetian red.

20: Der Wagen des Ares (Ares's Chariot). Only a few notes and fragments survive of this project for an 'aristophanic revue' centering on the god of war and his adventures (in the black market and elsewhere) following a military fiasco. Brecht had conceived it before leaving California, and was already counting on Neher for its realisation. Work began in 1948. The main legacy apart from a short ballet scenario is a dozen pen and gouache drawings by Neher (see p. 30) which show much the same gaiety and elegance as the *Courage* designs. They seem to have been made without thought of actual production.

VI. The Berliner Ensemble

Neher was with Brecht's East German company under the Intendantship of Helene Weigel from its formation in 1949 up to his final withdrawal in 1952. After that, his earlier designs still remained accessible to it, and he returned to collaborate with Engel on the 1957 production of *Galileo*, which he had already worked on with Brecht before his death. Besides the revival of *The Mother* in 1951 he did the sets for *Puntila* and *The Tutor*, co-directing the latter with Brecht, designed the unrealised *Days of the Commune* production and provided the sets for the State Opera's production of Paul Dessau's opera *Lukullus*. These last two works both ran into trouble with the authorities.

21: Mr Puntila and his Man Matti. Because of Neher's many commitments Brecht decided that he should not design the original Zurich production in June 1948, but a year later asked him to do the sets for its production by the brand-new Ensemble, and again in 1951 involved him

Mr Puntila and his Man Matti, the Berliner
Ensemble production by Brecht and Engel,
November 1949. Scene 9, the engagement
party, as conceived and as executed.

in the rejigging of this when Curt Bois – a very different type of actor: small, flexible and acrobatic – took over the name part from Leonard Steckel. The drawings, of which there are over 60 in the Brecht collection alone, date mostly from 1949. Stylistically they follow on from *Der Wagen des Ares*, making use of gouache and coloured paper, and giving every evidence of the artist's delight in the story and his imaginative engagement with its characters. Here are a number of the key incidents in the adventures of this split-character alcoholic-bucolic Finnish landowner and his dour chauffeur: from the opening session in the local hotel via the invitation and expulsion of the village women to the climax of the mountain peak on the billiard table – all just waiting (as Brecht found) to be copied on the stage.

22: The Days of the Commune. Like the *Ares* revue, this was a project which Brecht brought with him from America, intending to realise it as soon as he had found his feet. Neher will already have been aware of it in Zurich, where Brecht did much of the writing, and once again he committed himself imaginatively to its production, which was due to follow that of *Puntila* early in 1950. Some forty drawings are in the Brecht collection, ranging from scenes on the Paris barricades, at Versailles, in the Bank of France and the sittings of the Commune in the Hôtel de Ville, to sketches of the characters speaking, somewhat as for the 1931 *Man equals Man*. They show Neher at the height of his powers. By Christmas 1949 however the production had been stopped, allegedly because the Repertory Commission (one of a number of East German quangos then bedevilling the arts) considered Brecht's view of the Commune to be dangerously defeatist. The drawings remained unused, except when they were borrowed for a provincial production after Brecht's death: an act that naturally upset the artist.

23: The Tutor by Lenz. The adaptation by Egon Monk, Benno Besson and others of this remarkable eighteenth-century play was used by Brecht, after revision by himself, as a substitute for the indefinitely postponed *Days of the Commune*. As in the case of *Antigone* the production was jointly by Neher and Brecht, and clearly it was a very fine one, though there were only a few performances. Once again there are at least 40 drawings, now divided more or less equally between those in Brecht's collection and those which Neher took to Vienna. In a sense they seem more conventional than others of this phase in the artist's work, since both settings and costumes (the latter executed by Kurt Palm) are rooted in a traditionally-favoured period: the age of Goethe, Mozart and Sir Joshua Reynolds. They are none the less very different from Neher's

Two drawings for the cancelled Berliner
Ensemble production of *Days of the
Commune*, 1949/50.

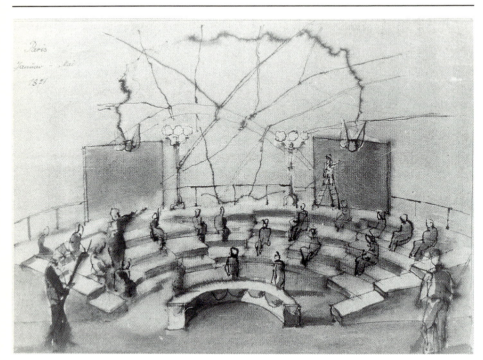

designs for the average German theatre or opera house, just as the play itself differs from the traditional norm. They are simply more alive.

24: Life of Galileo. It was at the end of 1955, only months before his death, that Brecht decided to go ahead with the production of *Galileo*, which he would co-direct with Erich Engel. Some of Neher's drawings are dated that year; one is dated 1951, suggesting that he and Brecht had already been talking about the play then; others are dated 1956; some not dated at all. The rehearsals, which began briefly in December and were resumed in spring 1956, were interrupted by Brecht's illness and came to a halt when he died. They were recorded on tape. Subsequently Engel carried on alone.

CASPAR NEHER *The staging of 'Antigone'*

In his new version of Sophocles's *Antigone* Brecht is trying to get rid of all mythological and religious bric-à-brac, feeling confident that such surgery will harm neither the great poem nor the old popular legends on which it is based.

This somewhat bold experiment led me for my part to dispense with certain (in my view) outmoded religious elements in today's theatrical conventions, particularly the miraculous way in which our stage and our acting technique conjure up the illusion that stage events are something real, in other words that a twentieth century audience can be led to believe that it is experiencing the stuff of legend, is living in Thebes, seeing the tyrant Creon and his great opponent Antigone, and so on. Accordingly I set the actors in full view of the audience and gave them just a small acting area between the old war posts within which to show how the characters in the poem conducted themselves. The same consideration led us to do away with the curtain, whose only function is to give the stage that quality of 'secrecy', 'magic', 'super-reality' which can be dispensed with once the acting is non-illusionistic. The ancients were no more familiar with the curtain than were the old German mystery plays or Shakespeare's Globe Theatre.

(1948)

Staging of *Antigone*, 1948. Concept and
realisation. The posts bearing horses' skulls
have been moved in to define the acting area,
leaving the actors' benches outside its
periphery.

BERTOLT BRECHT *Neher's stage for 'Antigone'*

Long benches, on which the actors can sit and wait for their cue, stand in front of a semicircle of screens covered in red-coloured rush matting. In the middle of these screens a gap is left, where the record turntable stands and is visibly operated; through this the actors can go off when their part is done. The acting area is bounded by four posts, from which horses' heads hang suspended. In the left foreground is a board for props, with bacchic masks on sticks, Creon's laurel wreath made of copper, the millet bowl and the wine jar for Antigone and a stool for Tiresias. Subsequently Creon's sword is hung up here by one of the elders. On the right is a framework with a sheet of iron on which an elder beats with his fist during the choral song 'Geist der Freude, der du von den Wässern'. For the prologue a white wall is lowered on wires. There are a door and a cupboard in it. A kitchen table and two chairs stand in front of it; a sack lies in the right foreground. At the beginning a board with the time and the place on it is lowered above the wall. There is no curtain.

The reason why the actors sit openly on the stage and only adopt the attitudes proper to their parts once they enter the (very brilliantly lit) acting area is that the audience must not be able to think that it has been transported to the scene of the story, but must be invited to take part in the delivery of an ancient poem, irrespective of how it has been restored.

There were two plans for the stage. The first was that the actors' benches should as it were represent the scene of the old poem. The screen behind them consisted of ox blood-coloured canvases reminiscent of sails and tents, and the posts with horses' skulls stood in between. The acting area was simply to be brilliantly lit and marked out by little flags. This would have represented a visible separation of the original poem and its secularised version. We became more and more dissatisfied with this plan, until we eventually decided to situate the new part of the story also between the barbaric war emblems. As a third possibility one could cut the prologue and replace the screens behind the benches by a board showing bomb damage in a modern city.

COSTUMES AND PROPS

The men's costumes were made of undyed sackcloth, the women's of cotton. Creon's and Hamon's costumes had inserts of red leather. Antigone's and Ismene's were grey. Particular care was taken over the props; good craftsmen worked on them. This was not so that the audience or the actors should imagine that they were real, but simply so as to provide the audience and the actors with beautiful objects.

(1949)

BERTOLT BRECHT *Stage design for the epic theatre*

We often begin rehearsing without any knowledge of the stage designs, and our friend merely prepares small sketches of the episodes to be played (for instance, six people grouped round a working-class woman who is upbraiding them). Perhaps we then find in the text that there are only five people in all, for our friend is no pedant; but he shows us the essential, and a sketch of this sort is always a small and delicate work of art. Whereabouts on the stage the woman is to sit, and her son and her guests, is something we find out for ourselves, and that is where our friend seats them when he comes to construct the set. Sometimes we get his designs beforehand, and then he helps us with groupings and gestures; not infrequently also with the differentiation of the characters and the way they speak. His set is steeped in the atmosphere of the play, and arouses the actor's ambition to take his place in it.

He reads plays in masterly fashion. Take just one example. In *Macbeth*, Act I, scene vi, Duncan and his general Banquo, invited by Macbeth to his castle, praise the castle in the famous lines:

> This guest of summer,
> The temple-haunting martlet does approve,
> By his loved mansionry, that the Heaven's breath
> Smells wooingly here. . .

Neher insisted on having a semi-dilapidated grey keep of striking poverty. The guests' words of praise were merely compliments. He saw the Macbeths as petty scottish nobility, and neurotically ambitious.

His sets are significant statements about reality. He takes a bold sweep, never letting inessential detail or decoration distract from the statement, which is an artistic and an intellectual one. At the same time everything has beauty, and the essential detail is most lovingly carried out.

With what care he selects a chair, and with what thought he places it! And it all helps the playing. One chair will have short legs, and the height of the accompanying table will also be calculated, so that whoever eats at it has to take up a quite specific attitude, and the conversation of these people as they bend more than usual when eating takes on a particular character, which makes the episode clearer. And how many effects are made possible by his doors of different heights!

This master knows every craft and is careful to see that even the poorest furniture is executed in an artistic way, for the symptoms of poverty and cheapness have to be prepared with art. So materials like iron, wood, canvas are expertly handled and properly combined, economically or lavishly as the play demands. He goes to the blacksmith's shop to have the swords forged and to the artificial florist's to get tin wreaths cut and woven. Many of the props are museum pieces.

Those small objects which he puts in the actors' hands – weapons, instruments, purses, cutlery etc. – are always authentic and will pass the closest inspection; but when it comes to architecture – i.e. when he builds interiors or exteriors – he is content to give indications, poetic and artistic representations of a hut or a locality which do honour as much to his imagination as to his power of observing. They display a lovely mixture of his own handwriting and that of the playwright. And there is no building of his, no yard or workshop or garden, that does not also bear the fingerprints, as it were, of the people who built it or who lived there. He makes visible the manual skills and knowledge of the builders and the ways of living of the inhabitants.

In his designs our friend always starts with 'the people themselves' and 'what is happening to or through them'. He provides no 'stage picture' to experience something in.

Almost all that makes up the stage builder's art he can do standing on his head. Of course Shakespeare's Rome was different from Racine's. He constructs the poets' stage and it glows. If he wants he can achieve a richer effect with a varied structure of different greys and whites than many other artists with the entire palette. He is a great painter. But above all he is an ingenious story-teller. He knows better than anyone that whatever does not further the narrative harms it. Accordingly he is always content to give indications wherever something 'plays no part'. At the same time these indications are stimulating. They arouse the spectator's imagination, which perfect reproduction would stun.

He often makes use of a device which has become an international commonplace and is generally divorced from its sense. That is the division of the stage, an arrangement by which a room, a yard or place of work is built up to half height downstage while another environment is projected or painted behind, changing with every scene or remaining throughout the play. This second milieu can be made up of documentary material or a picture or a tapestry. Such an arrangement naturally gives depth to the story while acting as a continual reminder to the audience that the scene designer has built a setting: what he sees is presented differently from the world outside the theatre.

This method, for all its flexibility, is of course only one among the many he uses; his settings are as different from one another as are the plays themselves. The basic impression is of very lightly constructed, easily transformed and beautiful pieces of scaffolding, which further the acting and help to tell the evening's story fluently. Add the verve with which he works, the contempt which he shows for anything dainty and innocuous, and the gaiety of his constructions, and you have perhaps some indication of the way of working of the greatest stage builder of our day.

(1951)

CASPAR NEHER *On the evolution of stage design*

When I set out full of enthusiasm to design for the stage I knew next to nothing about painting proper. This was an advantage, since I did not care for what I found and, like any normal young person, understandably wanted to do it better. At that time inflation in Germany was at its peak. Such was the economic background: theatres were still well enough off to permit experiments, and business people in general were more open to experiment than now, feeling no doubt that it was no longer possible to carry on along the old lines.

   Tairov arrived from Russia to demonstrate his theatre's stylistic experiments, making use of apparatus, traps, ramps and entrances for the actors; he trained his actors like variety artists who could dance and fence as well as speak. He was already experimenting with breaking out of the auditorium, doing away with the curtain; his theatre could function in a circus or in a hall [. . .]. In those days the Munich Kammerspiele was among the few theatres in Germany regularly presenting contemporary work. Those of us who had just been through the war could no longer feel very interested in Wagner's Elizabeth and her Hall of Song. However, one of those *Tannhäuser* productions at least achieved something by convincing us that it was time for a change. And change there was. Suppose things had been left as they were, we would have had the same kind of productions today, and there might have been no more Wagner. Maybe that was a mistake. But the Munich State Opera production was so appalling that one felt ashamed of having decided to take up stage design as a profession. Even my old teacher at the Academy quite justifiably shook his head: a symptom that long gave me food for thought.

   It was my lasting friendship with Brecht, then just beginning, that put me on the road which I cheerfully and uninhibitedly followed. I had already done a number of drawings for *Drums in the Night* and *Jungle*; *Baal* too was all there; and I hoped and believed that this would get me somewhere. The Kammerspiele had started preparations for *Drums in the Night*, and I went to the rehearsals.

There were also other circles that took an interest, such as that whose host and central figure was Lion Feuchtwanger, who liked to gather such talented young people as Erich Engel, Brecht and co. around him. That is where we used to meet and discuss the future of the theatre, which seemed no longer to be doing so well since the war. As the bourgeoisie grew more dominant the situation in the theatres gradually got worse; thus Steinrück resigned [as director of the Munich theatres after 1918]; politics reared its ugly head; violence began erupting; yet the personal courage of certain concerns was not to be broken. And since money was liquid on account of the inflation a fair amount of experimenting could still be done.

Drums in the Night was produced. Brecht brought Karl Valentin to the Kammerspiele on that occasion, a notable one since this was the beginning of Valentin's national reputation. Meanwhile we shifted our base to Berlin to look for openings there.

(Undated fragment).

CASPAR NEHER *Response to an enquiry about 'Das realistische Bühnenbild'*

I am afraid it is one of my principles to say nothing about that boring subject 'Realist stage design' or 'The realistic stage picture'.
At a certain distance the whole thing looks like a stupid fuss. Neither Hill nor anyone else has my permission to write anything whatever with regard to this theme.
> Best wishes,
> Neher

Unofficially. . .
Dear Bert,
How can you allow such letters to be written to me, letters that have to go straight into the wastepaper basket, just like in Goebbels's day? Then as now I used to be asked to say what I thought about Realist stage design. I didn't do so.

It means that there's no longer any point in working unless you put on blinkers first. And these have to be changed to suit the temperature. What's to become of thinking if nobody thinks the simplest things? A 'stage picture' is always real – that's already implicit in the Nazi term *Bühnenbild*.

Mightn't it be better to think a bit about the word itself? No other language talks about the 'stage picture'. *Scenografico* or *scenografica* is drawing the elevation of the stage. *Décor* is something else again, and comes a lot closer. *Stage designer* means a stage draughtsman, but no *picture*.

The words 'picture' and 'stage' are incompatible, except perhaps in the ballet. A picture is never realistic, the stage is always realistic. That's why I maintain that the 'realistic stage picture' is a nonsense. Nor can I imagine what can possibly be meant by it. A marble pillar can only be translated, i.e. at best hinted at; while if a turbine were a real one it would break the stage floor. This means that one always has to allow the audience to set their imagination to work in order to believe it could be a turbine, or might be a marble pillar. So you have to have an element of conjuring, of illusion. And in order to guide illusion along a track corresponding to some reality or other you may be able to dispense with reality itself. Perhaps reality is expressed in the proportions: a small house, a big hall, a stable and so on.

The young people on whom everything depends shouldn't learn from such articles how to construct a steam-engine, rather how such a machine *works* – that would be reality for you – how it starts, lets off steam, moves its connecting rod and so on. Too little attention is paid these days to the life of reality. The things we put on the stage are dead, never mind how real they are, if they have no function – if they are not used by the actors or used on their behalf. In other words we ought to be studying the environment; and then if we are *real*, all too real, we get back to atmosphere once more –

Things move in circles that are only too familiar. So the man who can get something from them is the one who knows how to use them, and [?that] their function in every play will be different. Setting up slogans as patterns to follow can only mislead people and cause endless confusion.

What have we been up to all these years except playing around with reality, [even where] it only needed to be suggested by a trouser-button or a telegraph pole? After all the moon too is a reality. It's not something we need to talk about.

I'm writing this in bed as that's the only spare time I get; I've been laid up with digestive troubles and so forth for a fortnight. It's hot out of doors.

All the best to Barbara. And to Helli. How about Venice? I wrote to Ballo about *Courage*. Giehse called. So did Viertel. They urgently *want* to talk to you about various

things. It would be a good idea if you came here. Not everybody can get to Berlin.
>All the best,
>as always,
>Cas.

(Undated. ?1951)

Early work. *Above*: Design (or illustration)
for scene 4 (iii) of *Baal*. Not carried out.
Below: For *In the Jungle*, 1923.? the present
scene 4.

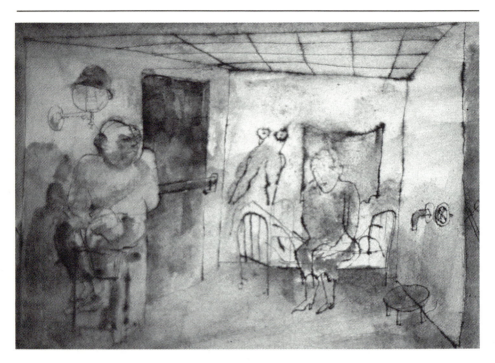

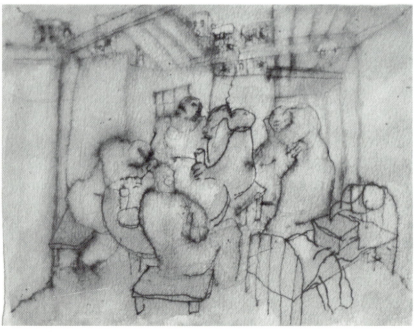

Designs for others – *their general pattern*

'Odeon Dancing Room', Early drawing for
an unidentified play.

Designs for others – their general pattern

I. The road to a modern theatre

When Neher moved to Berlin at the start of the 1924/25 season the fashion for Expressionism was over. Even Arnolt Bronnen, whose World War I play *Katalaunische Schlacht* had its première at Frankfurt in 1924 in one of Neher's earliest sets, was thought to be part of a new wave; so that Hasenclever's *Mord* at the Deutsches Theater was the only true Expressionist work that he designed. Max Reinhardt, who never cared for Expressionism, had moved to develop new projects in Salzburg and Vienna, leaving the Deutsches Theater to be run by others. Thus most of Neher's work there was under Engel's direction, and he only twice collaborated with the great impresario himself. With Reinhardt's main rival at the State Theatre however – Leopold Jessner – he worked a number of times; with Piscator (in the Weimar years) only once. Jessner concentrated mainly on the classics; Engel on formally conventional modern plays, especially those of Bernard Shaw.

1: With Max Reinhardt. The two productions which Neher designed were Klabund's *Chalk Circle* (1925) and Knut Hamsun's *Vom Teufel geholt* (at the Komödie in 1928). Elisabeth Bergner had one of her first great Berlin successes in the former, which was written by a friend of Brecht's and helped to inspire his own 'Caucasian' variant on the same Chinese theme. The Hamsun play had Oskar Homolka as one of its distinguished cast.

2: The Shaw experience. Starting with *You Never Can Tell* at the Deutsches Theater under Engel in 1925, Neher designed *Back to Methusaleh* and *The Doctor's Dilemma* in Berlin and *Major Barbara* and *Caesar and Cleopatra* in Essen, followed by further Shaw plays at the Deutsches Theater in the Nazi years: *Pygmalion* and *The Apple Cart* for Hilpert and *Man and Superman* and (again) *You Never Can Tell* for Engel to direct. Brecht's tribute (supposedly) for Shaw's seventieth birthday in 1926 will be found in *Brecht on Theatre*.

3: With Leopold Jessner. Though Neher's first Berlin job had been for Jessner's number two director at the State Theatre, Jürgen Fehling, he hardly worked for him again till after 1933. For Jessner himself however he designed ten productions, more than half of them after the beginning of 1930, when there was a strong agitation against Jessner as a Jew and a Social-Democrat. They included Goethe's *Egmont* and Schiller's *Jungfrau*

Neher's first major job: sets for Kleist's
Kätchen von Heilbronn at the State Theatre,
Berlin in February 1923.

Work for the Deutsches Theatre in the
1920s. *Above*: Max Reinhardt's production of
Klabund's adaptation of *The Chalk Circle*.
Below: Engel's production of Jules Romain's
Knock.

von Orleans and *Die Räuber*, as well as *Peer Gynt* (with Heinrich George as Peer) and Strindberg's *Gustav Adolf*, set like *Mother Courage* in the Thirty Years War. Perhaps the most memorable was Jessner's modern-dress *Hamlet* of 1926, for which Neher made some fine drawings. *King John* in 1929 was also done in a modern setting.

4: The 'Zeitstück' and political theatre. As the principal designer for Aufricht's management at the Theater am Schiffbauerdamm from 1928 on, Neher was close to the centre of the movement for 'theatre of the times', as it became called. That year he designed Lion Feuchtwanger's two 'Anglo-Saxon plays' about British India and the oil business respectively, both of them staged in the State Theatre, the first by Engel and the second by Fehling. In 1930 he designed the set for Reinhold Goering's play about Scott of the Antarctic which Jessner directed at the same theatre with projections by Nina Tokumbet. In 1929 he designed Lampel's anti-war play *Giftgas über Berlin* for the (largely Communist) 'group of Young Actors' to perform at Aufricht's theatre; it was banned after one closed performance. He also did his only job for Piscator – the sets for Maxwell Anderson's *What Price Glory?* – followed that summer by the Hecht/Macarthur *The Front Page* at the Berliner Theater, his first for Heinz Hilpert. He worked with Ernst Toller on the Schiffbauerdamm production of *Draw the Fires* – one of that year's three World War I naval dramas. All this would have made him suspect to the new nationalist reaction even without his close association with Weill and Brecht.

II. Opera in a changing Germany

Neher's opera experience – early and painful attendance at bad Wagner productions apart – dates effectively from the years 1927–28, when its triple foundation was laid. First came the most modern, up-to-date level with the concoction and performance of the 'Little Mahagonny' that spring; then a heavier stratum when he went to Essen and found himself designing Pfitzner's *Palestrina*; finally his first Büchner production in May 1928, when he came to grips with the classic author who inspired such composers as Alban Berg and Gottfried von Einem. Some of the operas which he subsequently designed – particularly those by Verdi and Mozart – became his stock in trade, to be re-staged in one theatre after another, often using the same scenic ideas.

5: The new opera and its successors. Following his close involvement in *Mahagonny*, Neher became both librettist and designer first for Weill's *Die Bürgschaft*, then for the four operas which Rudolf Wagner-Régeny

A design for Leopold Jessner's modern-dress
Hamlet at the State Theatre, December 1926.

From Neher's only job for Erwin Piscator,
Maxwell Anderson's *What Price Glory* in
1929.

wrote in the Nazi years, starting with the relatively successful *Der Günstling*. These works had in common, first, a static, cantata-like form which was not unrelated to the Bach Passions and the Brechtian 'Lehrstück'; and secondly a historical setting. Far less sensational at first hearing than some other contemporary operas, they were not very successful at the time and have remained somewhat underrated.

He also did a number of settings for Klemperer's radical Kroll Opera in Berlin, starting with an updated *Carmen* in October 1928. Subsequently he designed first productions for two of the more interesting composers of the Nazi years: Werner Egk and Carl Orff, starting with the former's *Zaubergeige*, which Oskar Wälterlin staged in Frankfurt in 1935. In 1937, when Wälterlin was preparing the première of Orff's *Carmina Burana*, Neher made various suggestions about the design, but left the actual work to Ludwig Sievert, somewhat to the composer's disappointment. He did however design the Hamburg production of 1942; and the two men were on 'Du' terms. Both also took refuge in a certain classicism which was not unsuited to the postwar Salzburg festivals.

6: The Büchner/Wedekind nexus. Berg's *Wozzeck* and the play *Woyzeck* on which it is based figure repeatedly in Neher's oeuvre, especially in the 1950s and 60s; and his various designs seem to relate to a common concept. He designed seven productions of the opera, starting with Essen in 1929 and including Covent Garden and the Metropolitan Opera, and six of the play, particularly for Oskar Fritz Schuh. *Danton's Death* he first designed for Essen in May 1928; in 1947 the opera version by his friend and ally Gottfried von Einem was performed in his sets at Salzburg. For Vienna in 1962 he designed Berg's *Lulu* opera – with Karl Böhm once again conducting, as for *Wozzeck* – but he had already designed the play version for Engel's Staatstheater production in 1926. Like Pabst's *Pandora's Box* film, this featured Fritz Kortner as Dr Schön.

7: Into the classic opera. It was when Carl Ebert arrived from Darmstadt, with Rudolf Bing as his administrator, to take over the Berlin Städtische Oper (now the Deutsche Oper in West Berlin) that Neher started to become known as a 'serious' opera designer. Having already worked with him on the première of *Man equals man*, Ebert asked Neher to design his first production there: Verdi's *Macbeth* in October 1931. *Ballo in Maschera* followed a year later, and before Ebert and Bing were purged by the Nazis early in 1933 they had also produced *Die Bürgschaft* and *The Flying Dutchman* with the same designer. Thereafter the connection was never broken, from *Carmen* in Vienna before the Anschluss through the Glyndebourne *Macbeth* in May 1938 to the same team's postwar produc-

From a lost scene for *Fear and Misery of the Third Reich*. 'The Gauleiter's birthday'.

tions at Glyndebourne, the Deutsche Oper (where they did *Falstaff* and a revised *Die Bürgschaft*), Covent Garden and the Met. In this way the Verdi operas became Neher specialities on the international opera circuit, much as did *Wozzeck*.

In Germany after 1933 he struck up a partnership with Walter Felsenstein at Düsseldorf and Frankfurt (*Traviata, Tannhäuser, Fledermaus*), which was briefly renewed at the East Berlin Komische Oper after 1945. In Austria following the Anschluss he started his long collaboration with Oskar Fritz Schuh, leading producer at Salzburg and the Vienna Opera for many years, and finally in Cologne; this covered both theatre and opera, and will be dealt with below. He also worked fruitfully with Josef Gielen at Dresden (e.g. *Don Giovanni* in 1935) and with such leading conductors as Karl Böhm and Fritz Busch. As a young man Herbert von Karajan conducted the Berlin première of Wagner-Régeny's *Die Bürger von Calais*, though subsequently Neher came to be somewhat critical of his style and judgement, particularly as overall artistic director of the Salzburg Festival in the late 1950s.

III. Theatre under the Nazis and its aftermath

8: Hilpert, Engel and the 'aryanised' Deutsches Theater. Heinz Hilpert, who had been an efficient middle-of-the-road director for Reinhardt before going to the Volksbühne in 1929, became the Intendant of the Deutsches Theater under Goebbels's Propaganda Ministry and subsequently of the Vienna Theater in der Josefstadt. From 1938 on, Neher designed some twenty productions for him, including *Twelfth Night, King Lear, A Midsummer Night's Dream, Antony and Cleopatra, A Winter's Tale* and the two Shaw plays, as well as standard German classics. These featured eminent if sometimes appallingly old-fashioned actors such as the bellowing Ewald Balser, who had once played the lead in the Düsseldorf première of *Man equals man*. At the same time Hilpert managed to get the authorities to allow an occasional production by Erich Engel, who had been working mainly in the cinema. Setting aside their memories of the 1920s, he and Neher now drew on much the same repertoire, starting with *Coriolanus* (played by Balser) in March 1937 and including *The Tempest, Othello, Man and Superman* and Calderon's *Dame Kobold*. They had not worked together for more than seven years.

9: The new Nazi plays. Though both Hilpert at the Deutsches Theater and Gustav Gründgens at Goering's State Theatre tried to avoid them, Neher designed a number of works by playwrights whom the Nazi

Two Nazi plays designed by Neher at
Darmstadt: above, Friedrich Bethge's *Pfarr
Pedr* (1941); below, E. W. Möller's *Der
Untergang Karthagos* (1938).

A successful conventional play, with set to match. The Zurich premiere of Carl Zuckmayer's *The Devil's General* 1946.

authorities particularly favoured. One of these was Walter Gilbrecht's historical play *Oliver Cromwell's Sendung*, which Hilpert staged at the Volksbühne in 1932, before the Nazi takeover. He also designed three plays by the Propaganda Ministry's E. W. Möller, starting with the première of his *Panamaskandal* at the Neues Theater, Frankfurt in October 1930; the others being *Struensee* (Frankfurt 1937) and *Der Untergang Karthagos* (Darmstadt 1938). In 1934 he designed the première of H. F. Blunck's *Land in der Dämmerung* at the State Theatre under Fehling's direction; in 1937 the Frankfurt production of *Gregor und Heinrich* by E. G. Kolbenheyer, president of the Chamber of Writers; in 1941 Friedrich Bethge's *Pfarr Peder* at Darmstadt. There is not much record of these productions.

10: The Zurich Schauspielhaus. This theatre, which had been the main centre of anti-Nazi theatre in the German-speaking world between 1933–45, was where Neher went as soon as he could leave Germany in 1946. Oskar Wälterlin, who had been one of the opera directors at Frankfurt during Neher's time there, took over the artistic direction in 1938; thus it was he who had accepted the three new Brecht plays which it staged during the war years. Brecht himself only arrived in the autumn of 1947. Meanwhile Neher collaborated with Wälterlin and Leonard Steckel on a number of productions, most notably designing the world première of Zuckmayer's *The Devil's General* (14 December 1946) under Hilpert's direction. Almost fourteen years earlier he and Hilpert had been responsible for the Volksbühne production of the same author's *Schinderhannes*, which opened just a week before Hitler became Chancellor.

IV. A world elsewhere

11: Fritz Kortner in Munich. When Kortner returned to Germany from the United States, where he had had no success as an actor in Hollywood, he came primarily as a director. In February 1953 Neher designed Tennessee Williams's *The Rose Tattoo* for him at the Munich Kammerspiele (with Maria Wimmer as Serafina), in 1955 Christopher Fry's *The Dark is Light Enough* and *The Lady's Not For Burning* at the same theatre and Shakespeare's *Julius Caesar* (with Paul Verhoeven and Ernst Ginsberg) at the Residenz-Theater. Among other productions designed by Neher at the Kammerspiele around that time were Greene's *The Power and The Glory*, dramatised by Dennis Cannan, and the young Peter Hacks's *Eröffnung des indischen Zeitalters* (with Steckel and Pamela Wedekind).

12: Revival and renewal of the Salzburg Festival. Neher's rôle in the planning of the first postwar festivals with Schuh and Von Einem is discussed above on p. 27. His responsibility as a designer was divided between the adaptation of performance spaces (such as the Residenz or the former 'Faust City' in the old riding school cut in the rock), the presentation of modern operas (to which the festival had traditionally been resistant) and the designing of the eighteenth century works, i.e. those by Mozart and Gluck. Nearly all his work was done with Schuh as director, and the Schuh/Neher/Karl Böhm Mozart productions with such singers as Schwarzkopf, Seefried, Jurinac and Erich Kunz were revived year after year throughout the 1950s. The modern operas were mainly West German or Austrian: two by Von Einem, two by Orff (including an *Antigonae* based on a somewhat different interpretation from Brecht's), two by Rolf Liebermann, one each by Blacher and Egk – and none by Wagner-Régeny who had settled in the GDR. Not one seems to have found a permanent place in the operatic repertoire. There were also plays by such authors as O'Neill and Fritz Hochwälder, while Neher redesigned the traditional *Jedermann*, which was staged on Reinhardt lines by Ernst Lothar. The Brecht *Dance of Death* never materialised.

13: The collaboration with Oskar Fritz Schuh. In quantitative terms Schuh was by far the most prolific director with whom Neher ever worked, not least because he worked as brilliantly in the theatre as in the opera house. The two men first met in the latter, when Schuh was directing Verdi's *La Traviata* at the Vienna Opera in 1940. Even under Nazi rule it seems that Vienna gave them a certain freedom (as it also did to Hilpert), and the première of the third Wagner-Régeny/Neher opera *Johanna Balk* the following year under Schuh's direction was an act of courage, since the theme – a dictatorial prince who is assassinated by his bodyguard – had made it unacceptable in metropolitan Germany. According to the composer arrests were made among the audience.

Thereafter it was Neher who helped Schuh stage Mozart in the Redoutensaal, the old Imperial ballroom in Vienna, and after the confusion of the immediate postwar months joined him in renovating the Salzburg Festival. Then in 1953 Schuh returned to the Berlin theatre as one of the directors of the (Western) Volksbühne, now performing in the Theater am Kurfürstendamm. Here, having already collaborated on Berg's *Wozzeck* for both Salzburg and Vienna, they produced the fine version of the original Büchner play which was seen in 1957 in London, as well as a wide variety of other classical and modern works – with the notable exception of anything by Brecht. After that Schuh, having lost his predominant rôle at Salzburg, became the Generalintendant – i.e. overall

Two episodes from the Stuart Webbs thriller
Der Meister. In 1921 Brecht and Neher tried
to write stories for this cliff-hanging series.

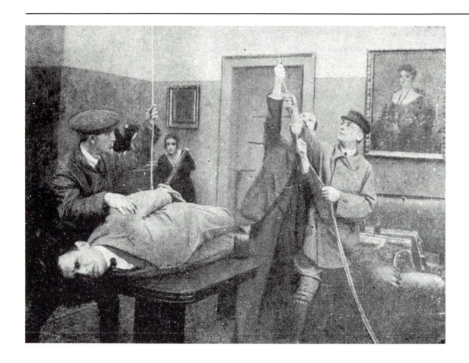

(1) Heinz Hilpert's *Die unheimlichen
Wünsche* (1939), after Chekhov.

(2) Two unrealised designs for DEFA's
frustrated *Mother Courage* project of the
1950s,
both featuring Yvette the camp whore.

director of both opera and theatre – in Cologne, where Neher continued designing for him in both branches. Closely as they saw eye to eye where the classic repertoire was concerned (and their correspondence deserves careful study) they never got beyond 'excellence', or managed to push the frontiers of the modern stage even as far as they had been pushed in the 1920s. It is difficult not to feel that for Neher Schuh was a congenial but relatively undemanding alternative to Brecht rather than a comparable creative stimulus.

14: Film and Television. After Pabst's *Threepenny Opera* film, which was Neher's only film job in connection with Brecht, he was involved in two other films. The first, in 1933, was directed by Fritz Wendhausen on the basis of Hans Fallada's Berlin novel *Little Man, What Now?*, with Hermann Thimig, Theo Lingen and other well known theatre actors. Robert Neppach produced. This was followed during the first winter of the Second World War by a Tobis film called *Die unheimlichen Wünsche* on a story by Balzac. Hilpert directed; Olga Tschechowa was the star. Neher's one TV job was the staging of Rolf Liebermann's opera *Die Schule der Frauen* in the eighteenth-century Schlosspark Theatre at Celle near Hanover for NWDR on November 30. This was Schuh's production, adapted for TV by Joachim Hess and Egon Monk.

15: Neher in the English-speaking world. Following the Volksbühne's London visit in 1957 – the year after the Berliner Ensemble's historic season at the Palace Theatre – Neher accused Schuh of claiming the credit for introducing him to the English public, when he had been well known to it ever since his Glyndebourne *Macbeth* nearly twenty years before. This was a slight overstatement. None the less nobody who saw that setting – even in a photograph – was likely to forget it, and his designs for Ebert's other productions after the Second World War were likewise memorable. Unfortunately the various efforts to show some of his designs at the New York Museum of Modern Art and other institutions in the United States all seem to have fallen through, and only a handful of his opera designs were shown there or in the United Kingdom. His creative contribution to the modern theatre has still hardly been understood.

BERTOLT BRECHT
The set

It's more important these days for the set to tell the spectator he's in a theatre than to tell him he's in, say, Aulis. The theatre must acquire quâ theatre the same fascinating reality as a sporting arena during a boxing match. The best thing is to show the machinery, the ropes and the flies.

If the set represents a town it must look like a town that has been made to last precisely two hours. One must conjure up the reality of time.

Everything must be provisional yet polite. A place need only have the credibility of a place glimpsed in a dream.

The set needs to spring from the rehearsal of groupings, so in effect it must be a fellow-actor.

Space needs to be brought to life in the vertical plane. This can be achieved by stairs, though not by covering those stairs with people.

On the time-scale the set must plainly become intensified; it must have its own climax and special round of applause.

The materials of the set must be visible. A play can be performed in pasteboard only, or in pasteboard and wood, or in canvas, and so on; but there mustn't be any faking.

(Mid-1920s)

BERTOLT BRECHT *Translating reality while avoiding total illusion*

I
A number of stage designers feel they have achieved their aim if you can look at their stage and believe you are in a real place in real life. What they ought to be doing instead is to make you believe you are in a good theatre. Or rather, they should make you believe you are in a theatre when you are actually in a real place in real life. For theatres are where you should learn a particular way of looking at things – a critical, attentive attitude to events, combined with a capacity to categorise ill-defined human groups according to the meaning of a particular event.

2
Theatre has a great deal to do with imitation. Just like actors, stage designers have to realise that imitation can only be a matter of one's imagination, that it has to comprise an element of change. Freedom on the other hand has to comprise an element of necessity.

3
The theatre has its own laws, and so long as these do not pretend to be more than laws they can be added to or revised at any point. The Chinese, for instance, indicate poverty by means of silken strips on their silken garments, suggesting rents and patches. The theatre has its own way of achieving seriousness. Not that its actual element of play is in any sense unserious; it just has continually to be kept in evidence. Thus a set representing extreme poverty or some highly dangerous situation can none the less include an element of ease, of light-heartedness. This relates to the Chinese principle for portraying the old, which is a thoroughly theatrical one, for it lays down that old men should be characterised mainly by

The 1926 matinée performance of *Life Story of a Man named Baal*, directed by Brecht and Homolka. Minimal design and its realisation.

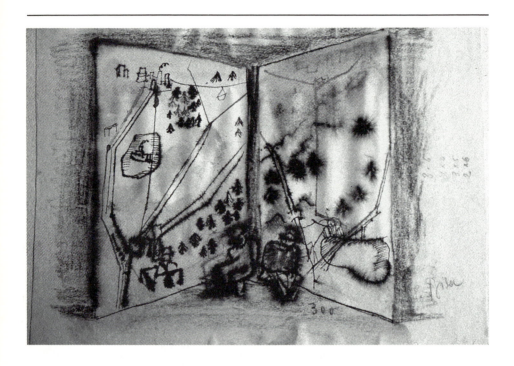

the inability of their limbs to obey them, yet that the portrayal itself must be fiery and powerful. A place's hideousness cannot be expressed by making the stage look hideous. That great stage builder Caspar Neher designed sets for *Life and Times of Baal the Asocial Man* – about the decline of a mere sensualist and his eventual incapacity to enjoy his senses – which implied the world's diminishing interest in such types by a flagrant display of indifference, to the point where towards the end a single brushstroke on a scrap of canvas had to suggest a wood. Here the theatre itself was providing the evidence of the loss of interest, though admittedly with the most splendid artistry. In such ways the stage designer can execute great instructive gests.

(Date uncertain. After 1930)

BERTOLT BRECHT *On the literarisation of theatres*

1

The stage builder must be able to think if he wishes to create art. There are times when it is less easy to think – i.e. to find ways out of one's difficulties – than at others where matters are not confused, and thinking becomes so simple that nobody notices it. In times when one section of humanity is confusing matters it often helps if thinking is made visible. So the stage needs to provide indications of the necessity of thinking.

2

This is where literarisation of the stage comes in. Sayings, photographs and images surround the character's actions. This is no less natural an environment than any other. Centuries of general reading have allowed inscriptions to assume the character of reality. In times when it is both necessary and difficult to create clarity, stage design can distance itself somewhat more from the other constituent arts of a theatrical performance than in other times, though it should maintain its independence even then. The stage designer can choose his own way of reacting to the events. However, the social task confronting him is the same as for the other arts.

3

Titles to prefix the scenes so that the spectator can move on from 'what' to 'how'; projections that stand in contrast to the events on stage; the disclosure of the lighting and musical equipment; the alienation of over-familiar locations so as to bring their social significance to the audience's notice – all these things will engender that attitude of realistic observation which is so essential in a world of deliberate confusion of concepts, of conscious and unconscious falsification of feelings.

The literarisation of the theatre. Evidently the screens in the 1928 *Threepenny Opera* were at first meant for projection of Neher drawings for each song, e.g. the 'Ballade of Good Living' and the 'Barbara Song' (*below*).

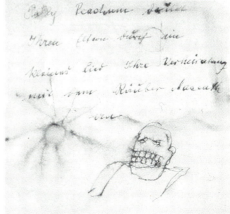

Neher's sketch for the finale (*above, right*)
shows how they might have looked. In the
event the writing of the titles, unlike that on
the curtain (*below*) was not in Neher's hand.

BERTOLT BRECHT
About starting from zero

Like the actors, the stage builder too tends to make the starting-point of his work too high. The right starting-point is point zero.

Instead of setting out by working up enthusiasm for the play, getting into the right mood, sketching out his visualisations or trying to think how far he can incorporate something he always wanted to do, he should make an effort to sober up, not to be enthusiastic so much as open-minded, not to seek sensations so much as to reflect.

One wall and one chair are already quite a lot. It is also quite difficult to get a wall straight and a chair properly on its legs. Suppose a factory yard has to be constructed, the stage builder ought to build it again and again, at least in his head, asking all the time: Is this a factory yet? Simultaneously he has to take account of the needs of the actors.

(Mid-1930s?)

EGON MONK
Neher and 'The Tutor'

Neher's room in the Berliner Ensemble building in the Luisenstrasse had nothing in it but a big trestle table of unpainted wood, a number of plain, rather rickety chairs and some space to walk around in. At the first discussion of a coming production he seldom took up his pencil. Brecht was the one who scribbled tiny plans or out-of-perspective views on scraps of paper, boxes, or backsides of manuscripts. Neher looked on in silence and turned them over. He would say nothing about a space till he knew what was supposed to take place in it. Similarly his scenic sketches (which were the second and most important step towards the eventual design), usually included no very exact indication of the décor. There might for instance be an open window with a woman leaning out of it, drawn in pen on dampened, tinted Ingres paper, without perspective and without space, as though the window were located in the paper. Or a door could open and a man leap through it, without there being any wall for the door to be in or any definite space for the man to enter. What mattered to Neher was exactly catching the scenic instant. Once he had got it he could elaborate the background much later.

Therese Giehse used to say that she found it impossible to learn her part by rote until she knew what attitudes the character she was playing was supposed to adopt in what situations. She was learning a character, not words. In the same way Neher's sketches anticipated a production by a particular director with particular actors and a particular Ensemble. They were not interchangeable, decorations for some production or other with conceivable alternatives. He was not sketching 'stage pictures' but the play.

This discussion about attitudes – or 'gests' as Neher, Brecht and their various disciples called, and still call them – was the main thing during the preliminary work on a pro-

duction and also at the ensuing rehearsals. Such discussions
were enjoyable. *Lustig*, in the sense in which Neher and
Brecht used the term. That is to say, free, full of ideas, open
to every conceivable aberration for the sake of finding the
right way, interrupted by laughter, shrouded in cigar-smoke,
open to anyone, including the youngest and least experienced
of those present, so long as he could work his passage by a
single pointed and entertaining formulation. 'Enjoyable' was
the highest term of praise offered by Neher-Brecht for a
comment, an observation, an insight or the acting out of a
scene.

It was truly enjoyable – as was half the production
that resulted – when Neher and Brecht, each trying to look
more inscrutable than the other, tried out Läuffer's bowings
and scrapings in the opening scene of *The Tutor*. Folding up
like a jackknife more and more profoundly before an imagin-
ary Major, scraping their feet so violently as almost to sprain
them, and all the while baring their teeth – for the poor
bastard is not scraping for pleasure. (Baring the teeth must
have meant something special during their long years of collaboration. It features in almost all Neher's sketches for the
Brecht plays). Following this performance, uproarious
laughter at Läuffer's obsequiousness. No sympathy for
creeps. Or Puntila walking across a big pub table, in the
belief that he is walking across the aquavit like Jesus across
the Sea of Nazareth. Aquavit buoys you up . . . Neher's
downward look of amazement after setting a first cautious
foot on the surface. He didn't sink! Or Brecht as Augusta
walking preoccupiedly into the lake, holding up his skirts as
prescribed, in order to commit suicide. And Neher's appalled
glance backwards, showing how intensely Augusta is hoping
that her rescuers will get there in time.

11
Brecht used to say of his work with Charles Laughton on
Galileo, 'As soon as L. heard of Caspar Neher's delicate stage

sketches, which allow the actors to group themselves according to a great artist's compositions and to take up attitudes that are both precise and realistic, he asked an excellent draughtsman from the Walt Disney Studios to make similar sketches'.

They always lay ready to hand on the director's table, with the scene currently being rehearsed on top. Nearly all the blocking of the Berliner Ensemble productions derived directly from Neher's sketches. If there was a particular scene, or a particular moment within a scene – a 'nodal point' as Brecht and Neher would call it – that had no sketch, or if Neher for once was not there (a rare occurrence in the first years of the Berliner Ensemble), then that rehearsal might well be broken off. As for instance when the last scene but one of *The Tutor* was being rehearsed: 'Engagement in a Snowstorm'. This had to appear as an idyll, amiable at first but gradually undermined by malice.

On stage, a large number of actors, glasses in their hands, drinking a toast (yes, but how?). Projected behind them, falling snow. Brecht rehearsed somewhat indecisively, asked first one then another of his aides to try blocking the scene, looked helplessly at the actors on stage, who looked equally helplessly down at him, then finally said: 'It's no use, we'll have to wait till Cas gets here.'

Unforgettable: Friedrich Maurer as Wenzeslaus the Schoolmaster in scene 11 of *The Tutor*. One hand holding Neher's sketch, the other holding the long quill pen with which the sketch shows him driving Count Vermuth and the Major's armed domestics from the room. A most impressive moment, clarifying the scene as no subsequent performance could do.

Occasional uncertainty. The drunken Puntila blessing his four fiancées: in Neher's drawing he has four arms. Where were the two extra arms to come from? Steckel invented a gesture that almost made one see Neher's four arms. Similarly Maurer's arm, correcting Läuffer as he ruled lines in

The Tutor, 1950. *Above*: 'Läuffer's bowings
and scrapings in the opening scene'.
Below: 'Friedrich Maurer as Wenzeslaus the
Schoolmaster in scene 11'.

his exercise books, seemed to get unnaturally elongated just like in Neher's drawing.

III

Brecht and Neher sitting next each other at rehearsal. Both of them leaning right back, their knees pressed against the seats in front. Brecht appreciatively studying his cigar; Neher, his eyebrows exaggeratedly raised or exaggeratedly frowning over his glasses, more severe. Assistants beside and behind them; guests at a distance. They are rehearsing 'by interjections'. Each interjection is prefixed by Neher or Brecht naming its originator. 'Neher thinks . . .', 'Besson thinks . . .', 'Brecht thinks . . .', 'Monk thinks . . .'. The interjection is listened to, then tested. If a detail works, then Brecht giggles with pleasure and Neher gives him a look of amusement; if it doesn't, the next interjection follows; if the idea was a mistaken one, but the best that can be thought up for a moment, then a profound silence sets in. This lasts a long time. The actors break off, walk around, wait for an idea to come to them, just like those below. Any guests not used to working patiently on themselves and the job in hand will be baffled. Is this a rehearsal, a break, or nothing at all? Again, some new actor, who has not been with the Ensemble long enough to shed his inhibitions and pomposity about the practice of his profession, may have heard a steady murmur building up from below as he performs a scene at full stretch. He stops abruptly, checks his gestures and turns ostentatiously towards the audience. This has absolutely no effect on the discussion going on in the stalls. In due course someone notices that the acting has come to an end. Amazed silence. Possibly the actor may say: 'If there's going to be all that noise of talking I shall walk out'. A pause, followed by the rasping voice used by Neher on such occasions: 'And stay out. It's the best thing you could do'. He could get extremely angry in this kind of situation. Weren't they working? And how could one work except by talking together? Just listening silently and watching would turn him into a mere consumer of what was being put before him on the stage.

Such a discussion might for instance lead to some new text. Brecht was very ready to rewrite, all too ready at times. Next morning there might be a little or a lot of paper for everyone, even just before the dress rehearsal. Neher's prompt book for the 1932 Berlin production of *Mahagonny* includes among a whole lot of plans the melancholy comment: 'Bert keeps bringing new text along every day, Kurt can't compose it in the time and proposes that the passages in question be read – so I'm putting up scaffolding either side of the gateway.'

IV
Costumes arrive and are checked over in the rehearsal room. Item by item. This takes a lot of time. Kurt Palm suggests, explains, alters, sends off, has variants brought along. Neher feels each material and each addition to it, rubs it between his fingers and adopts a sensual expression. He loves beautiful materials. He once called out to an actor 'How on earth can you treat paper like that?', then showed him how to approach paper. Lifting it gently as its lightness dictates, feeling its quality with his fingers, then taking it by the top with his other hand as he walked, so that the draught wouldn't crease it as he carried it across the stage.

Sometimes Neher appeared to have twinges of conscience when Brecht rejected some costume too promptly. He knew valuable materials weren't all that common in the place where he was. But usually he did not object. He shared Brecht's view that theatre is luxury. What a long time was spent experimenting with the blouse worn by Helene Weigel in *The Mother*. It was to be blue, but blue like calico that has been to the wash a couple of hundred times. Had it once had a pattern? Was this still visible? Had it picked up a blue or grey dye? Palm made tests and juggled the blouse through every conceivable stage. Luxury with unluxurious material. In the end it was the most beautiful blouse in theatrical history.

The furniture arrives. Wood is very special material in Neher's pictures. He studies table and chairs from the stalls. Can one see the top? If not, then the theatre's view is no better than the flat view of the cinema. Bring saws, cut those legs off. Now you can see the top. The actors sit round the table. But table and chairs don't create attitudes – it's not gestic. They're sitting any old how. Get out rods and rulers. Chairs and tables turn out to be standard height. Neher gives a rasp from the stalls. Someone says 'Cut them down to Neher-height'. Neher-height varies from one performance to the next, but is about 5 to 10cm below normal. It has become an accepted term for a particular measure in all those theatres where Neher and his assistants have worked. Similarly for years there has been a Neher make-up. It is so pale that the face appears undistorted, yet clearly distinguishable from the faces one sees in the interval in the foyer. A living mask.

Now the table is creating attitudes. One's back bends when one props one's elbows on the table, and one has to tilt one's head back in order to address one's neighbour. The actors are allowed to get up. Neher climbs up on the stage and grips the table. It's a small table in a small room lived in by poor people. Its boards haven't yet got those hollows that come from use and from continual scrubbing with sand. Neher walks round it sliding his hand along the edges. A lot of people have walked round this table in the same way, gripping its edges. They could be more rounded, worn down.

It was unusual for him to draw or paint during rehearsal. It was as if he valued his pen, ink, brushes and paper. If you want to alter a wall you only have to say how. It doesn't need to be drawn, no pen is needed. But if he did take up his brush it was quite a ceremony. He appreciated working. He took over small areas of the work like titbits; would stand alongside the scene painter, nodding to him now and again, and adding touches of gold to heighten the back-cloth for *Urfaust*. Economically, with a little black among the

Neher grey and Pompeian red. Unlike Brecht he didn't much
like being watched, but he could put up with it.

Neher was liable to get impatient if you didn't understand him, but he was patience itself at technical rehearsals
with Brecht. Brecht tinkered about with the lights, which
were never bright and white enough for him, complained
about unnecessary noise – though unnecessary noise is the
stage's accepted right at technical rehearsals – kept making
corrections, either real ones or to check furniture that he
claimed had been wrongly placed – and would shout at
people. Neher would hiss between his teeth, look downwards
instead of at Brecht (as a form of punishment), wait till
things quietened down, then take the next opportunity to
praise the victim. He made a distinction between the Bavarian
and the Prussian Brecht. Prussia, he claimed, was bad for
him; he would never have shouted in Bavaria.

Then he got up on the stage to check if Privy
Councillor von Berg's name had been spelt wrong on the
garden gate. The props man had followed Neher's sketch,
where of course it was spelt wrong. 'Von Berk', it said.
Neher was delighted. On being asked if the sign should be
corrected he grinned and waved the idea away. 'A few small
flaws add to the effect'. In scene 10 of *Puntila* there is a
painting that shows Puntila as a beast of prey alongside tiger,
crocodile, shark and vulture; over his head is the name 'Pun-
tilla'. and on the *Mahagonny* drawing with the measuring-
pole the name 'Begbick Street' is written 'Beckbickstr.'

V

The afternoon of the première is spent sitting idly around in
the stalls. The directors' table has been cleared away; one
feels lost. They try the curtains. Half-curtain open, half-
curtain shut, half-curtain open, half-curtain shut. It doesn't
billow the way it should. Neher makes an arm gesture to
show how it ought to billow. Two heavy lead balls are
removed from the hem on each side. Now it's billowing

more like it should, but the bottom isn't closing properly in the middle. Two lead balls are put in on each side. It's never going to billow quite like Neher's arm.

There's nothing more to be done. But one sticks around. Smoking heavily. No need to abstain like at the final rehearsals, and the firemen won't arrive for another couple of hours. Exceptionally, one recalls the past. Augsburg, for instance, so long as Brecht is absent. The Mahagonny man, who nowadays figures in the number 'God in Mahagonny', but already existed long before *Mahagonny*, even before the earliest Mahagonny songs. He used to hang on the cupboard in Brecht's room, a bowler hat on his head, his legs crossed à la Buddha, a big city beneath him.

Then Neher got up: time for the most important thing. For collecting his sketches, counting them, wondering if any had gone astray, turning a deaf ear to requests to be allowed to keep just one small minor one, finally picking up the whole bundle and personally locking it in his car. The première can go ahead.

(From Einem/Melchinger: *Caspar Neher*, 1966)

'Brecht and Bronnen', a drawing of about 1922, when the two young playwrights were plotting to assault Berlin with *Drums in the Night* and *Parricide* respectively.

A Neher chronicle

1897

11 April (Palm Sunday). Rudolf Ludwig Caspar Neher born Augsburg, son of Karl Wilhelm N., school teacher, and Maria Wilhelmine née Lembert, both of 4, Bismarckstrasse. Subsequently they have three daughters and another son, and move to 57 Kaiserstrasse, which remains their home until the 1920s.

1909

September. Neher enters the St Anna Humanistisches Gymnasium for a classical education.

1910

His first attempts at play-writing.

1911

September. He moves to the Real-Gymnasium, or secondary modern school, and is put in the same class (IVb) as the ten month younger Bertolt Brecht.

1914

July. Neher leaves school and briefly visits the Munich Kunstgewerbe- (or Applied Art) School.
August 2. Germany enters the First World War.
November 10. Brecht, in a letter, signs himself 'your brother *in arte*'.

1915

June 21. Having volunteered for the army, Neher is called up to the depôt of 4 Bavarian Field Artillery Regiment in Augsburg.
August 24. He is posted to 5 Battery, 1 Bavarian Field Artillery Regiment and serves in the battle of the Somme and on the Aisne and Artois fronts during 1915–16.

1917

January 26. Neher transfers to no. 218 Bavarian Close Combat Battery.

April 14. He is buried alive and evacuated to hospital in Alsace, where he remains till May 22 and makes a number of drawings. After reading Tolstoy's diaries he notes (in Latin) 'it is essential to paint; it is not essential to live'.
June–July. On leave and/or garrison duty in Augsburg and Munich, where he sees the annual art exhibition in the Glaspalast. He commissions Brecht to submit his work to the Kunstverein.
August 4. With 2 Battery, 4 Bavarian Field Artillery Regiment at Verdun, where he remains until the retreat begins in autumn 1918. From now on Brecht writes to him fairly regularly. One letter suggests he should do 'political stuff . . . large-scale, symbolic, à la Goya'. Another reports that Brecht has shown his drawings to *Simplizissimus*, who like them but find them not topical enough. Meanwhile Neher is sending drawings from the front to Brecht.
November 7. 'October Revolution' in Russia.
December 16. Neher becomes a non-commissioned officer.

1918

February 2. Neher is awarded the Iron Cross, Second Class.
March. In various letters Brecht describes Wedekind's death and his own intention to write a play about Villon – which by June has materialised as the first version of *Baal*. He has also written some songs to the guitar for Neher to illustrate. He asks Neher's advice about his own impending call-up: should he become a gunner or a medical orderly? Neher replies flippantly.
November 9. 'November Revolution' in Germany. Abdication of William II. Proclamation of Bavarian Soviet Republic.
November 11. Germany signs the armistice on the Western Front. Neher's unit begins the march back. By the 14th it

has reached Baden, and he notes that 'the whole lot is on the march – home is like a magnet . . . Everyone's glad the swindle has ended . . . Golden sunshine lights our road home . . . All are wearing red'.

1919

January 5–11. Spartacist Rising in Berlin.

January 16–19. Neher is accepted as a student at the Munich Academy by the illustrator Angelo Jank. He celebrates with Brecht and other friends at the 'Karpfen' dance hall in Augsburg. Two nights later Brecht sings his new songs at Gablers Taverne.

February 2. The army discharges Neher as a Lance-Sergeant.

February 13. Brecht has finished *Drums in the Night*, his play about the Spartacist Rising. Neher notes that he is seeing Brecht whenever possible.

February 26. They join the funeral procession for the murdered Socialist Kurt Eisner. Two nights later they see Strindberg's *Dance of Death 1*, with Tilla Durieux and Albert Steinrück.

March 5. Neher has been making drawings for *Baal*. He now calls on Emil Pirchan the stage designer and asks if he can work with him in the summer vacation.

April 20. Counter-revolutionary troops take over Augsburg. Neher tells his father he won't join them.

May 2. Fall of Munich Soviet. Landauer and Leviné murdered, Toller gaoled.

May. Brecht, Neher and his sister Marietta visit the Augsburg 'Plärrer' fair (with its swingboats). Revision of *Baal*, which is submitted to Musarion (publishers) with Neher's illustrations. By July they have rejected it. The friends continue seeing much of each other all summer.

August 2. Neher is godfather to Brecht's illegitimate son Frank Banholzer.

1920

January. He is still seeing much of Brecht in both Munich and Augsburg. Further revision of *Baal*; further illustrations by Neher.

February. Lion Feuchtwanger has shown his drawings to Pasetti, chief designer to the Bavarian State theatres, and to Falckenberg, director of the Munich Kammerspiele, who like them and are prepared to help him. Neher and Brecht dislike Pirchan's sets for *Der gerettete Alkibiades* by Georg Kaiser. They see Sternheim's *1913*. *Baal* is sent off to the publisher Georg Müller, who takes it to proof stage before getting cold feet. In mid-month Neher asks to transfer to the painting department of the Academy under Ludwig Herterich. He admires El Greco, Grosz, Klee but Herterich is conservative. Brecht visits Berlin and recommends Neher to do likewise.

Summer. Brecht working on *Galgei* (first version of *Man equals Man*) and the revision of *Drums in the Night*. Excursions with Neher and others to the Bavarian and Würtemberg countryside. Some disagreements, reflected perhaps in Brecht's poem 'Fat Caspar' (in his diary for September 5th).

1921

February 9. Neher visits the Steinicke Gallery in Munich with the Feuchtwangers and Brecht.

February-March. He makes designs for *Drums in the Night* and collaborates with Brecht on a film story about pirates. This is followed by 'The Mystery of the Jamaica Bar' which they hope to sell to the Munich producers of the Stuart Webbs detective series. Neher is attending lectures on Cézanne, but Brecht thinks his painting has 'gone romantic'.

Spring-Summer. They discuss Marées. Work on the *Galgei* project and another film story, 'Three in a Tower'. Neher copies a Rubens to make money after the painter Max Unold has criticised his work.

November 7. Brecht to Berlin, where he

remains till the following spring and completes the first version of *In the Jungle*.

1922

Neher gets engaged to Erika Tornquist from Graz (Austria), sister of his fellow-student Martin Tornquist. He decides to concentrate on stage design. First contract with the Munich Kammerspiele.

End April. Brecht returns from Berlin. In Moscow Meyerhold stages *The Magnificent Cuckold* with Constructivist setting by Popova – a landmark in modern design.

Summer. Preparations for staging of *Drums in the Night* at the Kammerspiele. Neher's designs are rejected in favour of the theatre's newly-appointed designer Otto Reigbert. Erich Engel from Hamburg persuades the Residenz-Theater to produce *In the Jungle*. One of his Munich productions attracts favourable notice in Berlin.

September 29. Première of *Drums in the Night*. The critic Herbert Jhering gives Brecht the Kleist prize, which opens all theatres to him. He becomes a dramaturg at the Kammerspiele.

December 2. *Drums in the Night* opens at the Deutsches Theater, Berlin – this time with sets by Pilartz.

1923

Year of the great inflation. Unsettled situation in the theatres, with some closures, formation of short-lived actors' companies and a general feeling that Expressionism has run its course.

February 1. Opening of the first production designed by Neher. This is Kleist's classic *Kätchen von Heilbronn,* which Jürgen Fehling has directed for the Berlin Staatstheater with Carl Ebert and Ernst Legal in the cast. In Munich Brecht and Feuchtwanger plan a Shakespearean production which Neher is to design. Initially they pick on *Mac-beth*, but later change to *Edward II* by Marlowe.

May 9. Première of Brecht's third play, *In the Jungle* (first version), which Engel directs at the Munich Residenz-Theater with sets and costumes by Neher. Neher does dozens of designs and illustrations. This is his first work with Engel.

August 18. He marries the nineteen year-old Erika Tornquist in Graz, where her father is Geology professor at the Technische Hochschule.

Autumn. Work on *Edward II,* including illustrations for its publication by Kiepenheuer.

November 7–8. Hitler's 'beer-cellar putsch' in Munich.

December 8. Long-delayed première of *Baal* in the Altes Theater, Leipzig under Alvin Kronacher's direction. Paul Thiersch is the designer.

1924

February 29. Engel directs *Danton's Death* at the Deutsches Theater in Berlin, where he has been engaged as senior director (Oberspielleiter) by Reinhardt's stand-in Felix Holländer. Kortner plays Danton.

March 18. Première of *Life of Edward II (after Marlowe)* by Brecht and Feuchtwanger, directed by Brecht at the Munich Kammerspiele, with Homolka as Mortimer. Neher provides a wealth of drawings for sets and costumes, and scores a notable success.

Summer. The Nehers and the Brechts holiday in Italy, visiting Capri and Positano. The director Bernhard Reich and his Lithuanian wife Asya Lacis join them. Back in Augsburg, Brecht resumes work on *Galgei*.

September. Exodus from an increasingly stagnant Munich. Holländer engages Neher on a two-year contract, and Brecht too joins the Deutsches Theater as a junior director for one year. Others who now move to Berlin include Feuchtwanger, Reich, Horváth and Tol-

ler (following his release from gaol).
October 14. Birth of the Nehers' son
Georg. Three weeks later Brecht's son
Stefan is born to Helene Weigel, his
second wife.
October 29. *Jungle* opens at the Deutsches
Theater with sets and costumes by
Neher. Engel is the director and
Kortner plays Shlink.
December 4. Fehling directs *Life of
Edward II* at the Staatstheater, Berlin in
sets by Rochus Gliese, with Werner
Krauss as Mortimer.

1925

February 27. Engel's production of *Coriolanus*, with Kortner in the title part,
opens at the Lessing-Theater. Neher is
the designer and Brecht has attended the
rehearsals. The critic Jhering sees this
and the Munich *Edward II* as pioneer-
ing a new treatment of the classics.
Summer. Neher visits Paris. 'Neue
Sachlichkeit' exhibition at Mannheim
provides name for the general trend
towards sobriety and functionalism in
the arts.
October 20. Klabund's *Kreidekreis* (Chalk
Circle, or Circle of Chalk) is directed
by Reinhardt at the Deutsches Theater
with Elisabeth Bergner in the lead and
sets by Neher.
End of year. Brecht completes the
reworking of *Galgei* as *Man equals Man*
with the help of Elisabeth Hauptmann.
Its location is transferred from Bavaria
to British India.
December 22. Zuckmayer's vastly successful *Der fröhliche Weinberg* (the cheerful
vineyard) paves the way for a new
popular, middlebrow theatre.

1926

January 8. Engel's Deutsches Theater production of the *Lysistrata* opens.
Designer: Neher.
February 14. *Baal*, reworked and greatly
shortened, is staged by Brecht and
Homolka for a single performance in
screen-like sets by Neher at the

Deutsches Theater. Weigel plays Lupu.
Brecht is much occupied with the
theory of 'epic theatre' as practised by
himself and by Erwin Piscator, now
chief director for the Berlin
Volksbühne.
June. Neher and Brecht in Paris.
Autumn. Neher becomes staff designer for
the Staatstheater.
September 25. Dual première of *Man
equals Man* at Darmstadt Landestheater
and Düsseldorf Schauspielhaus. Neher
designs Jacob Geis's production at the
former, using the Brechtian half-curtain.
Ernst Legal plays Galy Gay.
October 22. Neher has designed Engel's
Staatstheater production of Wedekind's
two *Lulu* plays.
December 3. Has designed Jessner's
modern-dress production of *Hamlet*
(Kortner) at the Staatstheater.

1927

March 18. Radio broadcast of *Man equals
man* leads to Brecht/Weill collaboration
and first discussions about a 'Maha-
gonny' opera. The first fruits are some
'Mahagonny songs'. For Hindemith's
summer music festival at Baden-Baden
they link these in a 'Songspiel' known
as *The Little Mahagonny*, for which
Neher designs projections. Brecht
develops his concept of 'separation of
the elements'.
July 17. Single performance of the
'Songspiel' at Baden-Baden directed by
Brecht on a boxing-ring stage.
Début of Lotte Lenya. Well received by
Otto Klemperer and Hans Curjel of the
Berlin Kroll Opera.
Autumn. Neher goes to the newly
reconstructed Essen City Theatres as
head of design, with Hein Heckroth as
his aide, Hannes Küpper as dramaturg
and editor of 'Der Scheinwerfer' and
Martin Kerb as director of plays. In the
first year he designs eight opera produc-
tions and eleven plays, i.e. roughly two
productions a month. Meanwhile in
Berlin Piscator opens his first

independent season, with Brecht as one of his dramaturgs.

October 14. Brecht's radio adaptation of *Macbeth* is broadcast from Berlin.

October 15. Fehling stages Elsa Lasker-Schüler's *Die Wupper* at the Staatstheater, with Neher's sets.

December 10. *In the Jungle of Cities* (revised) is staged by Carl Ebert at the Darmstadt Landestheater, but Neher is not involved.

1928

January 5. *Man equals Man* is staged by Engel at the Berlin Volksbühne with Neher as designer and Helene Weigel playing Begbick. Brecht meantime is involved with Piscator's *Schweik* production for which Grosz has provided cut-out figures and an animated film.

June 12. Feuchtwanger's India play *Kalkutta 4 Mai* at the Staatstheater is directed by Engel and designed by Neher. The music is by Hanns Eisler, who has set Brecht's 'Ballad of the Soldier' for it.

Summer. The Nehers drive to the south of France, where Brecht and co. are working on an adaptation of *The Beggar's Opera*, cross to Algeria and return via north Italy.

Autumn. At Essen Heckroth takes over as head of design, but Neher remains committed as a guest designer. He designs seven operas in the following year, and *Wozzeck* at the end of 1929.

August 3. Première of *The Threepenny Opera* (as the adaptation is now called) at E. J. Aufricht's Theater am Schiffbauerdamm in Berlin. This most successful of all Brecht/Weill/Neher works runs for a year and has productions throughout Germany, often re-using Neher's designs.

October 31. The Kroll Opera puts on *Carmen*, directed by Legal and designed by Neher, who designed the same opera for Essen six weeks earlier. Their regular head of design is Teo Otto.

November 28. Neher and Weill are involved in the première of Feuchtwanger's second 'Anglo-Saxon Play' *Die Petroleuminseln*, which Fehling directs at the Staatstheater.

1929

First quarter. In addition to his work at Essen Neher designs the banned *Giftgas über Berlin* and Marieluise Fleisser's *Pioniere in Ingolstadt* for Aufricht. The second, featuring Lenya and Peter Lorre, is directed by Brecht and Jacob Geis. Both plays are strongly anti-army.

April 12. Rudolf Wagner-Régeny's short operas *Moritat, Moschopoulos* and *Sganarelle* are performed at Essen with sets by Neher.

May 1. Police action against the Communists in Berlin leads Brecht to commit himself to the latter, though without joining their party.

Summer. The Nehers spend the holiday touring Jugoslavia. The rest of the *Threepenny Opera* team are in the south of France again, planning a successor.

Autumn. Economic and political crisis. This is marked by the death of Gustav Stresemann, the adoption of a harder line in the USSR and the Wall Street crash. From now on the Nazi party is a force to be reckoned with, steadily gaining seats at all kinds of election. There is a growing reaction in the arts.

August 31. Première of *Happy End* at the Theater am Schiffbauerdamm by the old team, now reinforced by Lorre, Homolka and Carola Neher, is a failure, due partly to Brecht's interest in new didactic forms. Neher begins a contract with the Volksbühne, where Heinz Hilpert from the Deutsches Theater is now Intendant. Collapse of Piscator's second company with *The Merchant of Berlin*.

September. Neher designs triple bill of short operas by Ravel, Milhaud and Ibert for the Kroll Opera. Zemlinsky conducts and Gustav Gründgens directs.

November. At Essen Neher designs the

nationalist play *Flieg, roter Adler von Tirol.*

1930

January 22. *Man equals Man* at Essen Stadttheater, apparently using Neher's Berlin designs.

March 9. Première of *Rise and Fall of the City of Mahagonny,* the full opera version, at the Neues Theater in Leipzig under Walter Brugmann's direction. Neher's projections are henceforward an integral part of the work, which is greeted with protests by Nazis and the Nationalist right. The Kroll Opera in Berlin, which was hoping to stage it, decides that it cannot afford to.

March 30. Start of rule by Presidential decree.

April. Meyerhold's Moscow theatre gives a short season in Berlin.

Whitsun. The Nehers tour Spain, returning via Bordeaux-Paris and Belgium.

Summer. Start of work on G. W. Pabst's film of *The Threepenny Opera,* for which Andreiev does the sets and Neher the costumes.

Autumn. Work for Frankfurt and Essen as well as the two naval dramas by Toller and Friedrich Wolf in Berlin.

1931

February 6. Under Legal's Intendantship Brecht directs *Man equals Man* at the Staatstheater with Lorre as Galy Gay and Weigel again as Begbick. Neher designs the skeletal set and the larger-than-lifesize soldiers, and provides Brecht with projections and drawings of the action. Sergei Tretiakov sees this very short-lived production as comparable with Meyerhold's *Cuckold* of 1922. The music is by Weill.

February 19. Première of Pabst's *Threepenny Opera* film.

May 29. Neher has designed the Kroll Opera's last production, Janáček's *From the House of the Dead.*

1932

January 17. Première of *The Mother* at the

Komödienhaus, with Weigel in the title part.

March 10. Première of the Weill/Neher opera *Die Bürgschaft* at the Städtische Oper, conducted by Fritz Stiedry and directed by Ebert with designs by Neher. Evidence of Nazi and anti-semitic hostility, though critics are favourable.

April 11. Brecht's *Saint Joan of the Stock-yards,* which has prompted drawings by Neher but is rejected by the Volksbühne and other theatres, has its only performance for the next 25 years – a broadcast by Berlin radio with Kortner as Mauler.

June 1. Franz von Papen becomes Chancellor. He denounces 'cultural bolshevism'.

Summer. Holidays in Graz and Augsburg.

July 20. By presidential decree Papen dissolves the Socialist-led Prussian government, which is responsible for the arts and the Berlin police.

September 28. *Ballo in Maschera* at the Städtische Oper, directed by Ebert and designed by Neher.

Autumn. *Die Bürgschaft* is performed at Wiesbaden under Karl Rankl and Düsseldorf under Horenstein. Five other productions of it have been called off.

December. In Paris Neher designs Curjel's trimmed-down production of *Mahagonny* at the Salle Gaveau, which introduces Weill and his collaborators to France.

December 22. He has designed Hilpert's Volksbühne production of *Oliver Cromwell's Sendung* by the nationalist playwright Gilbricht.

1933

January 30. Hitler becomes Chancellor.

February 18. Première of the Weill/Kaiser opera *Silver Lake* at the Altes Theater, Leipzig. Director, Detlev Sierck; designer Neher.

February 27. The Reichstag Fire is followed by a wave of arrests. The Brechts drive to Prague; Neher drives the Weills to Paris.

April 13. *The Threepenny Opera* opens at the Empire Theatre, New York, with Lenya and Louis Armstrong. Neher's designs are realised by Cleon Throckmorton.

April 20. Hitler's birthday is marked by a production of Johst's Nazi play *Schlageter* at the Staatstheater. The cast includes Emmy Sonnemann, shortly to become Mrs Goering.

Spring. Edward James's 'Ballets 1933', with Abravanel as conductor and Balanchine as choreographer, commission Weill and Brecht to write *The Seven Deadly Sins*, for which Neher will design sets and costumes. It is performed in June, with Lenya and Tilly Losch as the two Annas, at the Théâtre des Champs-Elysées and the Savoy Theatre, London (where Constant Lambert conducts). Subsequently Neher returns to Germany while his friends start their twelve years of exile. At first he is forbidden to work there, but by the end of the year he has designed a production for the Volksbühne, which Martin Kerb stages on November 27.

1934

First half. Seven productions at various theatres, including the première of *Land in der Dämmerung* by the Nazi H. F. Blunck, which Fehling stages at the Staatstheater on April 13. In England in May the first Glyndbourne Festival is held in John Christie's private opera house, with Ebert as artistic director and Rudolf Bing as talent scout.

Autumn. Neher is taken under contract by Hans Meissner, the new Frankfurt Intendant, whose leading directors are Oskar Wälterlin and Walter Felsenstein. By autumn 1938 he has designed 35 productions for them, mainly of operas. The first of these is *Tannhäuser* staged by Felsenstein, which opens on September 26. Neher also works on his libretto for Wagner-Régeny's *Der Günstling*,

based on Victor Hugo's *Mary Tudor*. In August he meets Weill in Verona.

1935

February 20. Première of Wagner-Régeny/ Neher *Der Günstling* at Dresden Opera, conducted by Karl Böhm and directed by Josef Gielen with sets by Neher.

March 25. An unidentified official tells Goebbels Neher is too 'compromised' by his collaboration with 'the notorious Jewish composer' Weill, to be head designer at the Volksbühne.

May 22. Première of Werner Egk's opera *Zaubergeige* at Frankfurt. By the end of July Neher has designed ten productions in all, most of them in Frankfurt and Düsseldorf.

Autumn. This continues at the rate of a production a month, culminating in Frankfurt's Christmas operetta, *Die Fledermaus* directed by Felsenstein. During the same year Neher visits Zurich and Salzburg, and meets Weill, who is relieved that he has not been 'gleichgeschaltet' (or forced into conformity). Brecht goes to Moscow (where he is invited by Piscator, now heading the International Organisation of Revolutionary Theatres) and to New York. He is deprived of his German citizenship.

1936

Besides regular productions for Frankfurt and Düsseldorf (where Küpper directs *Maria Stuart* at the end of the year) Neher does *Carmen* for Dresden and the dialect play *Datterich* for Goering's Staatstheater under the Intendantship of Gründgens.

1937

First half. Besides Frankfurt, where he is beginning to lose interest, particularly after Felsenstein's suspension by the Propaganda Ministry, and Düsseldorf, Neher now designs for the Dresden Opera (*Macbeth* on May 12) and the Hamburg Schauspielhaus. He also returns to the Deutsches Theater, which under Hilpert has become a rival to the Staatstheater.

March 26. There he designs Erich Engel's *Coriolanus,* for which Wagner-Régeny writes the music. It seems that Hilpert has won them some kind of licence to do an annual Shakespeare production.

Autumn. Hilpert engages Neher as a regular designer for the Deutsches Theater, where he does 41 productions in all up to the theatre's closure in 1944. In December Neher designs *Carmen* for Ebert's production at the Vienna State Opera, which is not yet under Nazi control.

1938

February 28. Shakespeare's *The Tempest,* directed by Engel and designed by Neher, opens at the Deutsches Theater.

March 13. Hitler annexes Austria.
This leads to purging of the Salzburg Festival and the Vienna Opera; likewise emigration of Reinhardt, Zuckmayer and others, and takeover of the Theater in der Josefstadt by the Deutsches Theater.

May 31. Ebert's production of *Macbeth* opens at Glyndebourne, with sets by Neher.

September 29. Munich Agreement allows Hitler to annex Czech frontier areas.
Autumn. Neher designs five productions, of which three are for the Deutsches Theater.

1939

January 28. Première of the Wagner-Régeny/Neher opera *Die Bürger von Calais* at Berlin State Opera, with sets by Neher and Karajan conducting.

February 19. Neher's father dies in Augsburg, aged 81.

March 15. Germany occupies rest of Czechoslovakia.
April 6. Shakespeare's *Othello* at the Deutsches Theater, directed by Engel, designed by Neher.

September 1. German invasion of Poland launches Second World War.
October 7. *Twelfth Night* at the Deutsches Theater, directed by Engel, designed by Neher, music by Wagner-Régeny. It transfers to the Theater in der Josefstadt on November 3.

1940

Of six productions for the Deutsches Theater designed by Neher during the year, three are plays by Shakespeare – *King Lear* on March 9, *A Midsummer Night's Dream* on September 9 and *Richard II* on November 30. According to Goebbels's 'Reich Dramaturg' this last was cleverly directed by Hilpert so as to criticise the 'Anglo-Saxon-plutocratic ruling caste'. He praised Neher's and Wagner-Régeny's contributions.

December 19. The sets for *La Traviata* at the Vienna Opera inaugurate Neher's long and close collaboration with the director Oskar Fritz Schuh.

1941

Of fourteen productions designed by Neher five are for Vienna, three being for the opera and two for the Theater in der Josefstadt. Four of the rest are for the Deutsches Theater. The operas include the Wagner-Régeny *Johanna Balk* which had been rejected by the Berlin State Opera as an 'impossible work' not to be performed within 500 km of Berlin. It opens on 4 April with Schuh directing and Leopold Ludwig conducting. Schuh and Neher also collaborate on the adaptation of the Redoutensaal for performances commemorating the 250th anniversary of Mozart's death.

In December Neher begins a regular collaboration with the Hamburg State Opera, for whom he designs fifteen productions over the next five years. He works particularly with Alfred Noller.

December 21. Death of Neher's brother Ernest on the south Russian front.

1942

Neher designs five productions for Hilpert in Berlin or Vienna, and three for the Vienna Opera. He seems to be returning to painting. His summer holiday is spent in Italy.

October. He designs Orff's *Carmina burana* for the Hamburg Opera.

1943

German armies withdraw from Africa and surrender at Stalingrad.

Neher works on *Der Darmwäscher*, his next libretto for Wagner-Régeny, and designs six operas for Vienna, Hamburg and Frankfurt, all from the standard repertoire. His son Georg, a medical student aged twenty, is posted to an engineer unit on the Russian front and on April 8 is reported missing near Nikolaev. No more is heard of him. In November Brecht's son Frank (Neher's godson) is killed near Porchov. There are heavy air raids on Berlin.

1944

Neher designs three operas and two plays before all German theatres are closed on August 25. Eleven days before that date Hilpert is denounced to the Propaganda Ministry for having said that he had met none but decent Jews. On November 1 he is drafted to war work at Telefunken where Neher too has been sent. Thereafter Neher, now aged 47, is detailed to various airfields before going to the Air Ministry film service.

1945

March 22. Neher moves to Hamburg, where he helps rebuild the Opera once war is over.

May 8. Final German surrender concludes the war in Europe. Hitler and Mussolini are dead, the Red Army in Vienna and Berlin.

Summer. Unable to get travel permits, Neher is stuck in Hamburg. Of his closest allies, Wagner-Régeny is in Berlin, Schuh in Vienna, Hilpert in Switzerland, Brecht in California, where he is preparing the translation and production of his *Life of Galileo* with Charles Laughton. Weill is an established composer of Broadway musicals.

November 15. *Fidelio* is performed in Munich with Neher's designs – seemingly his only production this year.

1946

First half. Neher designs eight productions in Hamburg State Opera and Schauspielhaus.

April 19. Leopold Lindtberg's second production of Brecht's *Mother Courage* opens at Zurich Schauspielhaus, with sets by Neher. (The first, exactly five years before, was designed by Teo Otto, the theatre's resident designer).

Spring. Brecht gets Neher's (Hamburg) address from Hermann Kasack, and wants to resume collaboration. Neher turns down Hamburg's offer of a long-term contract.

Summer. Under three successive annual contracts he works for the Zurich Schauspielhaus, where Wälterlin has been directing the best and most resistant of all the anti-Nazi German-language theatres. By the end of May 1949 he has designed nineteen productions for them. He lodges at Pension Delphin, Iris-Strasse. His sister Margarete Berber is at Salem on Lake Constanz.

Autumn. Brecht writes suggesting 'a few years' working together in Switzerland or North Italy. Brecht would like to use the Theater am Schiffbauerdamm in Berlin, with Geis perhaps in charge of it.

December. Further letters from Brecht in California say he will insist on the use of Neher's designs for any production of his plays in Germany. He has sent food parcels and offers other help. Hopes to come to Switzerland in June 1947, and says he has been told (in confidence) that he may use the Theater am

Schiffbauerdamm 'for certain matters'.

December 14. Zuckmayer's *The Devil's General*, written in American exile, has its première at the Zurich Schauspielhaus. Director: Hilpert. Designer: Neher. It is one of the great postwar successes.

1947

January 6. Ernst Ginsberg stages Brecht's *Fear and Misery of the Third Reich* in its original prewar version at Basel, with projections by Neher.

Jan-Feb. Neher is invited to design *Rigoletto* for the Cambridge Theatre, London, and to collaborate with Ebert at Glyndebourne. For the Scala, Milan he designs Britten's *Peter Grimes* (première March 11).

Early April. He meets Ebert to discuss work. His designs are used for the Glyndebourne *Orfeo* in June.

July 10. The American Chief of the Theater Control Section for Bavaria reports that Neher has been 'thoroughly cleared politically'.

Summer. First job for the revived Salzburg Festival. Neher designs Schuh's production of *Danton's Death* by the Austrian composer Gottfried von Einem, a friend of Wagner-Régeny's (première, conducted by Ferenc Fricsay, on August 6). The three collaborators henceforward play a leading role in the Festival, for which Neher continues working annually until the 1960s. Already in August they are discussing the Austrian conductor Herbert von Karajan, formerly a Nazi supporter.

September 18. Neher and Ebert meet in Zurich, where the former has four plays to design.

November 1. Two days after his hearing by the Un-American Activities Committee in Washington, a month before the opening of Laughton's *Galileo* in New York, Brecht lands in Paris.

November 5. The evening of his arrival in Zurich, where he plans to stay for a year, Brecht meets Neher at the Hotel zum Storchen. They continue to meet daily until the end of the month, when they start work on a joint production of the Hölderlin *Antigone* for the small theatre at Chur managed by Hans Curjel. Brecht rewrites the text, which he prefaces with a prologue set in the ruins of postwar Berlin. Neher designs costumes and set. Helene Weigel plays Antigone, her first professional part for ten years or more. Neher and Brecht direct.

1948

February 15. *Antigone* opens at the Chur Stadttheater, where Schuh and Von Einem see it. There are four performances in all, followed on March 14 by a single matinée performance at the Zurich Schauspielhaus. Neher, Schuh and Von Einem discuss Brecht's possible involvement in the Salzburg Festival.

Spring. Neher goes to Milan for the production of *Parsifal*, which he has designed for La Scala. On his return he and Brecht discuss the latter's satirical revue project *Der Wagen des Ares,* for which Neher makes many drawings. He also makes designs for *Puntila*, though by May it seems clear that he will not have time to carry them through, and Brecht asks Teo Otto to take over. Before leaving for Salzburg at the end of that month he again discusses Brecht's involvement there. By now Von Einem has suggested Brecht's applying for Austrian citizenship as a step towards this.

May 22. *King Lear*, designed by Neher, opens at the Zurich Schauspielhaus.

June 5. Première of *Puntila* at the same theatre, directed by Kurt Hirschfeld and (anonymously) by Brecht in Otto's sets.

June 24. Russians blockade land routes to West Berlin.

Summer. At Salzburg Neher adapts the 'Felsenreitschule', the arcaded former riding school where Reinhardt regularly staged *Faust*, with a view to its use for opera productions. The first of these is Gluck's *Orpheus*, which opens on July 28. With his colleagues he discusses instituting an opera course, to be directed by himself, Von Einem and Curjel.

Autumn. Neher designs *Carmen* for Vienna and *Figaro* for Milan. In November he is granted Austrian citizenship. Brecht completes the writing of his theoretical work the 'Short Organum', and goes to Berlin for the production of *Mother Courage*. This is to take place in the Deutsches Theater, now in the Soviet sector of the city, which is directed by Wolfgang Langhoff from the Zurich Schauspielhaus. Weigel will play Courage. On the way the Brechts see Von Einem and Erika Neher in Salzburg.

1949

First half. Neher designs five productions for the Zurich Schauspielhaus, including both parts of Goethe's *Faust*. He cannot join the *Mother Courage* team, though Brecht and Engel press him to. The immense success of this production, which Engel directs in sets by Heinrich Kilger based on Teo Otto's 1941 arrangement, leads to a project for a 'Berliner Ensemble' to be led by Brecht and Weigel and accommodated provisionally by the Deutsches Theater. Weigel remains in Berlin while Brecht returns to Zurich to recruit for the company. At the same time he writes to Von Einem that he wishes to apply for Austrian citizenship, which he formally does on April 20.

April 22. An updated version of *The Threepenny Opera* opens at the Munich Kammerspiele with Hans Albers – an actor popular throughout the Third Reich – as Macheath. Harry Buckwitz directs, using designs by Neher. It is not a success.

May 23. Setting up of West German state, followed by East German (October 7).

Summer. At Salzburg Neher helps stage

The Magic Flute and Carl Orff's *Antigonae* in the 'Felsenreitschule'. Brecht returns to Berlin, but is in Salzburg at the end of August to discuss his idea for a *Salzburg Dance of Death* inspired by the Basel carnival, which would provide an open-air production comparable to the Hofmannsthal/Reinhardt *Everyman* which was at the heart of the festival before 1938. Neher for his part is to be the regular head of design for the new Berliner Ensemble, starting with the impending production of *Puntila*.

August 21. Ebert's production of *Ballo in Maschera* opens at Glyndebourne, using Neher's designs. Subsequently it goes to Bing's Edinburgh Festival.

Autumn. The Nehers return to their Berlin house in Zehlendorf: Zinsweilerweg 16, which has survived the bombing. Neher contracts to work for the Ensemble from 1 Sep to 31 Oct and 1 Feb to 31 March. Brecht agrees to the East German DEFA making a film of *Mother Courage*.

November 8. At the Deutsches Theater the Berliner Ensemble opens with *Puntila* directed by Brecht and Engel and designed by Neher. Several of the company are from Zurich, notably Steckel, Giehse and Lutz.

December. Brecht's *The Days of the Commune*, which was to have been his next production, is held up by the East German authorities. Instead he works with Neher on an adaptation of Lenz's eighteenth-century *The Tutor*.

1950

January. Neher is under contract to work on the *Mother Courage* film project till the end of the month. He designs *The Mother* for Leipzig, followed in February by *Puntila* for Dresden (both major East German cities). For the Vienna Burgtheater (playing in the Ronacher) he designs *Richard II*. It opens in March, directed by Berthold Viertel.

April 10. Brecht too is granted Austrian nationality.

April 15. Première of *The Tutor*, directed by Brecht and Neher with costumes and sets by the latter. Hans Gaugler (Creon in the Chur *Antigone*), plays the lead.

Spring-Summer. Brecht discusses the unfinished Wagner-Régeny/Neher opera *Der Darmwäscher*. At Salzburg Neher designs *Don Giovanni* in the 'Felsen-reitschule' and two productions in the Landestheater. On 20 July he turns down Helene Weigel's offer of a further contract with the Berliner Ensemble.

October. In East Berlin Neher designs a double bill for Felsenstein at the Komische Oper. Brecht meanwhile is in Munich, directing *Mother Courage* for the Kammerspiele. He tells Von Einem he will write the *Salzburg Dance of Death*, and suggests that *The Caucasian Chalk Circle*, as yet unperformed, might be produced at the festival with Homolka as Azdak.

November. Neher designs two productions for Boleslav Barlog's Schlosspark-Theater in West Berlin. For the Berliner Ensemble he next works on Brecht's production of *The Mother*.

1951

January 12. *The Mother* opens at the Deutsches Theater, with Weigel as Vlassova and Busch as Lapkin. Brecht directs in sets by Neher, with projections by Heartfield and his brother. It is a less austere and to some extent a more 'realistic' production than that of 1932.

Jan–March. Brecht and Paul Dessau are much concerned with the latter's opera *Lucullus*, which Legal at the State Opera (in East Berlin) is committed to produce. Neher is to be the designer. Eventually there is a trial performance in the Admiralspalast on March 17, after which President Pieck and the cabinet persuade them to make changes diluting the total pacifism of the script. Meanwhile Neher designs *Freischütz* for Felsenstein.

Summer. From Munich, where he designs Eliot's *The Cocktail Party* for the Kam-

merspiele, Neher goes to Italy, returning to Salzburg for the festival. On August 16 *Wozzeck* is performed with his sets in the reopened Festspielhaus. At the end of that month he travels back to Berlin, where he has a contract to design for Barlog at the Schlosspark and the (more important) Schiller-theater. In the meantime the Salzburg authorities and the Austrian Ministry of the Interior have come under attack for granting citizenship to the pro-Communist Brecht. Von Einem has had to resign from the festival board.

October 12. *The Condemnation of Lucullus*, revised version of Dessau's opera, opens at the State Opera. Hermann Scherchen conducts, Wolf Völker directs; the design is Neher's. After this he is more or less simultaneously working for Barlog, designing *Egmont* for Frankfurt and helping Brecht re-rehearse *Puntila* with Curt Bois taking over the title part.

December 6–8. Neher briefly visits London, where he is to design *Wozzeck* for Covent Garden. Much of the work has already been done, as have drawings for Verdi's *La Forza del Destino* in Vienna.

1952

Jan–Feb. *La Forza del Destino* opens in Vienna on January 15, followed by the Covent Garden *Wozzeck* a week later and a further *Wozzeck* in Vienna a fortnight after that. Neher is then involved in the preparation of the Berliner Ensemble *Urfaust*, which is designed by Hainer Hill. It eventually opens on April 23. Subsequently Helene Weigel is ordered to take it out of the repertory.

February 23. She offers Neher a contract as 'Künstlerische Beirat' (or artistic adviser) from 1 Feb–30 Apr and 1 Sep–30 Nov. This is to cover the designing of Shakespeare's *Coriolanus*, on whose translation and dramaturgy Brecht has been working since November. Neher sends it back at the end of the month, having already done a number of drawings.

Mid–March. Neher, who has been hoping for a professorship at the West Berlin Academy under Carl Hofer, is told that he is disqualified by his Austrian nationality and his work with Brecht.

March 28. Première of Pogodin's *Kremlin Chimes*, which Busch has directed with the Berliner Ensemble. Neher is appalled by the play and by Heartfield's conventional sets for it. He sees this as 'the end of the Berliner Ensemble'.

June–August. After the opening of Wedekind's *Lulu*, which he has designed for Barlog, Neher goes to Switzerland for a fortnight before the Salzburg Festival. He designs the revival of *Jedermann* on the cathedral square. Then from mid-August till his return to Berlin he is mainly in the Bavarian Alps apart from some ten days in Italy.

July. *Macbeth* is staged by Ebert at Glyndebourne using Neher's designs.

September 23. Neher arrives in Berlin from Italy, to hear from Hainer Hill that Brecht has been railing against those members of the Ensemble who refuse to live in East Berlin. On the 25th he drafts a letter to Brecht explaining that he has been advised by Hilbert of the Austrian Ministry of Education to stop working in East Berlin altogether, since this is now regarded as 'political activity' incompatible with his citizenship oath. He asks Brecht to understand this 'abominable situation'.

November 18. Hill telephones Neher in connection with Brecht, after which there appears to be a break in communication.

1953

January. Brecht decides that the *Mother Courage* film project is 'hopelessly bogged down'.

First half. Neher designs only four productions: plays for Barlog and the

Munich Kammerspiele, and two operas for Vienna. From March 7 he spends about a month travelling in Italy and painting, the high point being a visit to Paestum.

June 16–17. Following Stalin's death there are riots in Berlin and East Germany. Brecht incurs odium in the West for his support of the GDR government.

Summer. At Salzburg Neher designs three productions, including Von Einem's new opera *The Trial* after Kafka's novel. This is subsequently performed in the Vienna State Opera.

Autumn. Schuh, who is the new artistic director of the West Berlin Volksbühne (in the Theater am Kurfürstendamm), makes Neher his regular designer. In the next five years Neher designs 22 productions there, starting with Büchner's *Woyzeck* which opens on December 23. He nonetheless proposes to leave Berlin at the end of the 1953/54 season, apparently in order to move house to Munich.

1954

During this year Neher is responsible for sixteen fairly routine productions in theatres in Berlin (Schiller-Theater and Volksbühne), Hamburg, Munich, Zurich, Salzburg and Vienna. On May 15 he signs a three-year contract as head of design at the Munich Kammerspiele under Hans Schweikart, but leaves his job at the end of the 1954–55 season, during which he designs six productions. In East Berlin the Berliner Ensemble moves into the Theater am Schiffbauerdamm, where Karl von Appen becomes its principal designer.

December. The Salzburg Festival committee ask Neher to join their new 'Kunstrat', or artistic board. Von Einem becomes chairman, and other members are Schuh, Herbert Graf, Ernst Lothar and the chairman of the Vienna Philharmonic.

December 21. Brecht is to be awarded the international Stalin Peace Prize.

1955

During the year Neher designs twenty
productions for much the same theatres
as before.

April 18. Death in Munich of Neher's
mother, aged eighty-five.

April 28. Brecht and Neher meet at the
Munich Kammerspiele.

June 27–30. They see each other daily in
Zurich, where Neher has designed the
production of *The Good Person of
Szechwan* at the Schauspielhaus.

August. Filming of *Mother Courage*
begins at the DEFA studios, but is soon
broken off, partly because of Brecht's
objections to the heavy Hollywood-
style sets. Neither Neher nor Engel are
now involved. The director is Wolfgang
Staudte. The project is abandoned.
Meanwhile at Salzburg the artistic board
of the festival holds its first meeting. It
objects to the proposed long-term contract with Karajan, and votes against
granting him plenary powers over the
staging. Neher appears to be threatening
to leave.

November 19. Sam Wanamaker writes
from London, asking if Neher will
design his forthcoming production of
The Threepenny Opera at the Royal
Court Theatre.

December. Brecht, despite bad health,
starts working on the Berliner Ensemble's production of *Galileo*, of which he
has made a third version. (The first was
staged by the Zurich Schauspielhaus in
1943, the second in Hollywood in
1947). Neher prepares designs.

1956

A crucial year in the English theatre.
George Devine's English Stage Company takes over the Royal Court
Theatre, which sees the première of
Osborne's *Look Back in Anger*, initiating a new, ungentlemanly type of
actor and play.

January. Neher makes further sketches for
Galileo.

February. Two influential productions of
The Threepenny Opera. At the Piccolo
Teatro in Milan Strehler stages it in sets
by Teo Otto. At the Royal Court
Wanamaker uses Neher's designs. On
the 15th Brecht gives a party in Berlin,
which Neher attends. On the 20th
Neher goes to England for a week to
join Günther Rennert and Hans
Schmidt-Isserstedt, who are advising the
Earl of Shrewsbury about the possibility
of creating a 'Midlands Glyndebourne'
at Ingestre Hall.

March 21. Baron Puthon, chairman of the
Salzburg Festival, tells Von Einem that
Karajan is being made overall artistic
director for three years. Karajan's con-
dition, it appears, is that Von Einem
should be got rid of.

March–April. At the Schiller-Theater
Neher works – apparently for the first
time – with Piscator, who is directing
Danton's Death. He is frequently tired,
and his doctor reports circulatory problems. Disagreements with Piscator lead
him at one point to resign, but his name
remains on the programme.

May. Brecht breaks off his rehearsals of
Galileo for health reasons and goes into
the Charité hospital. The Berliner
Ensemble begins preparing its forthcoming visit to London, where Peter
Daubeny has invited it to take part in
the World Theatre season. Neher, who
finds himself 'getting visibly thinner',
leaves for a month's holiday in Italy,
and meets the painter Werner Gilles on
Ischia. He returns to the Bavarian Alps
before going to Salzburg.

July 28. The artistic board, centering on
Von Einem, Schuh and Neher, and sup-
ported by Hilbert, meets in Salzburg,
but is ignored by the Festival authorities. Subsequently Von Einem ceases to
be chairman, and in November Neher
writes to the Landeshauptmann (provincial premier) withdrawing from the
Festival after two singers have refused
to wear his *Figaro* costumes.

August 14. Neher, on the move between

Italy and Bavaria, is bowled over by the news of Brecht's death from a coronary in Berlin.

August 27. The Ensemble open their three weeks' season at the Palace Theatre, London, with the Brecht/Engel production of *Mother Courage*, in which Weigel plays the title part. Neher's work is not represented.

September. Neher returns to Berlin and confers with Engel, who is taking over the Ensemble's *Galileo* production. He subsequently gets a formal contract for designing the sets and costumes.

September 30. George Devine's production of *The Good Woman of Setzuan* opens at the Royal Court Theatre, with Peggy Ashcroft as Shen Te, Devine as the barber and John Osborne as the carpenter. It has been designed by Teo Otto, as the company could not afford Neher's fees.

October 7. Neher writes to Elisabeth Hauptmann telling her of his private understandings with Brecht. These include a share of the *Antigone* rights and the preservation and cataloguing of his drawings for the Ensemble. She confirms that he gets a fifth of Brecht's royalties on the former.

October 24. In Hungary Imre Nagy becomes premier and is ousted by the Red Army.

October 31. Anglo–French bombing of Egypt starts the brief Suez War.

November. Without previous consultation, Neher's old *Days of the Commune* designs are being used for Benno Besson's production of the play at Karl-Marx-Stadt (the former Chemnitz). He is told that this is intended as a pilot production for the Ensemble.

November 20. Neher is asked if he will succeed Emil Pirchan as professor of stage design at the Vienna Academy of Fine Arts. In mid-December he agrees.

December 9. Verdi's *Ballo in Maschera* at the Städtische Oper, director Ebert, designer Neher.

1957

January 15. Erich Engel's Berliner Ensemble production of *Galileo*, with Neher's sets and Eisler's music, opens at the Theater am Schiffbauerdamm. Neher meanwhile is on his way to Stuttgart, where he is designing Handel's *Jeptha* for the Landestheater with Günther Rennert as director.

February. A new contract for the Salzburg Festival offers him increased control of the workshops and an extra 3000 Schillings. The Berliner Ensemble are staging *Fear and Misery of the Third Reich* but his projections are set aside in favour of documentary film clips. The scenes are allotted to individual young directors.

Spring. Neher visits Italy.

Summer. Having signed the new contract for the Festival, Neher designs two productions for the Salzburg Landestheater. From June 17-22 the Theater am Kurfürstendamm company under Schuh are in London, where they perform Büchner's plays *Woyzeck* and *Leonce und Lena* with Neher's sets and costumes.

October 6. The Weill/Neher *Die Bürgschaft* is revived by the Berlin Städtische Oper with Arthur Rother conducting and direction by Carl Ebert.

December. Ebert and Rudolf Bing are arranging to bring Neher to the Metropolitan Opera, New York.

1958

January–March. The Met. engage Neher to design *Wozzeck* and *Macbeth*, for fees and expenses totalling about $13,000. He is required briefly at the end of March, but the main work will be next winter.

Spring. He is formally appointed professor at the Vienna Academy, where he is to begin teaching in the autumn. He and his wife sell their Berlin house and move to Vienna, living at first with his brother-in-law Richard Zeltner in the 19th District.

Summer. At Salzburg Neher is involved in four productions.

Autumn. He is not engaged in any
theatre.
November 14. Erich Engel announces his
intention to direct *The Threepenny
Opera* with the Berliner Ensemble, and
asks Neher to design it once again. In
the event the job is done by Von
Appen.

1959

Jan–Feb. Neher is in New York for the
Met.'s productions of *Macbeth* (opening
February 6) and *Wozzeck* (opening
March 3).
April 30. About thirty years after Brecht
and Neher began working on it, the
former's play *Saint Joan of the Stock-
yards* has its première at the Hamburg
Schauspielhaus. It is designed by Neher
and directed by Gründgens, to whom
Brecht first offered it in 1949.
Summer. At Salzburg Neher designs H.
Erbse's opera *Julietta*. It has been
accepted on the recommendation of
Von Einem, who has always wanted the
Festival to support new works.
Unfortunately it is not a success.
Autumn. Schuh has become General-
intendant of the Cologne theatres, and
renews his collaboration with Neher
there. Looking back, he feels that Von
Einem made mistakes and that Karajan,
while still on a different wavelength to
Neher and himself, has behaved
correctly.
December 9. In Vienna the Nehers move
into an apartment of their own at
Kreindlgasse 25 in the 19th district.

1960

During the year Neher is responsible for
twelve productions, three of them in
Hamburg, five in Cologne and two at
the Salzburg Festival. Rolf Badenhausen, one of the Cologne dramaturgs,
organises a comprehensive exhibition of

his work in the Wallraf-Richartz
Museum in that city from 2 Apr to 22
May. It includes some paintings, and is
subsequently shown at the Academy in
Vienna.

1961

Seven productions during the year, two of
them for Cologne and the remainder for
different theatres. Neher has decided
not to go to Salzburg, where he does
not care for the new developments and
the moneyed audience. He thus misses
the première of Wagner-Régeny's new
opera *Das Bergwerk zu Falun*. In a letter of February 19 he advises Wagner-
Régeny against staying near Salzburg
and says he is 'better off living in
Thuringia' away from transistor radios.
May–June. The Berliner Ensemble are
preparing a production of *Coriolanus* in
Brecht's translation, and correspond
with Neher about it. Weigel suggests
that if he does not wish to carry
through the project himself they should
ask Von Appen to execute his earlier
designs 'in line with your ideas'.
September. After many years of digestive
troubles, which the doctors ascribed to
thyroid hyperactivity, Neher, now aged
64, is told that he must be operated on.
November 23. He has the operation in the
university clinic at Freiburg im
Breisgau.

1962

Neher dies in Vienna on June 30, followed
on September 24 by his wife Erika. Six
productions designed by him are seen at
various German and Austrian theatres
in the course of the year, but his last
work appears to be the pen drawings
for Von Einem's still unperformed
opera *Der Zerrissene*, based on a play
by Nestroy.

Two pen drawings. *Above*: A rehearsal of
The Tutor, showing Brecht in cap, left.
Below: Scene in a bar, from the collection of
Hainer Hill.

Cover design for Lion Feuchtwanger's
pseudo-American poems *Pep* (1928).

Bibliography *and list of exhibitions*

1. Writings by Neher

Die Bürgschaft (Opera by Kurt Weill). Universal-Edition, Vienna, 1932.
Der Günstling oder Die letzten Tage des grossen Herrn Fabiano (Opera by Rudolf Wagner-Régeny). Universal-Edition, Vienna, 1935.
Die Bürger von Calais (Opera by Wagner-Régeny). Universal-Edition, Vienna, 1938.
Johanna Balk (Opera by Wagner-Régeny). Universal-Edition, Vienna, 1941.
Persische Episode or *Der Darmwäscher* (Opera by Wagner-Régeny). Piano score, Universal-Edition, Vienna, 1951. Numbers 4, 15 and 18 have texts by Brecht.
R. Wagner-Régeny, Caspar Neher: *Begegnungen*. Discursive recollections and journal extracts by the former, with letters by both. Henschel-Verlag, East Berlin, 1968.

2. Collaborations

'Suggestions for the stage realisation of the opera *Rise and Fall of the City of Mahagonny*', with Kurt Weill, 1929. In Brecht: *Collected Plays* volume 2 iii, Eyre Methuen, London, 1979.
Antigonemodell 1948, with Bertolt Brecht. Gebrüder Weiss, Berlin, 1949. Foreword under title 'Masterful treatment of a model' in *Brecht on Theatre,* below.
Radetzkymarsch, with Egon Monk. (Stage adaptation of the novel by Joseph Roth). Duplicated script, Kiepenheuer & Witsch, Cologne, 1955.

3. Monographs

Gottfried von Einem and Siegfried Melchinger (eds.): *Caspar Neher.* Bühne und bildende Kunst im XX. Jahrhundert. Friedrich-Verlag, Velber bei Hannover, 1966. Comprehensive work with 24 colour plates, many black and white illustrations, writings on and by Neher, a 56-page annotated list of productions and other apparatus. The colour plates appeared separately from the same publishers a year later with the main essays by Melchinger and Teo Otto, under the title *24 Farbtafeln zum Heraustrennen und rahmen.*
Franz Hadamovsky: *Caspar Nehers szenisches Werk.* Ein Verzeichnis des Bestandes der Theatersammlung der Österreichischen Nationalbibliothek. National Library, Vienna, 1972. Full catalogue of Neher's 'Nachlass', with introduction and chronology. Some line illustrations.
Max Högel: *Caspar Neher (1897–1962).* Sonderdruck aus *Lebensbilder aus dem Bayrischen Schwaben.* Anton H. Konrad Verlag, Weissenhorn, 1973. 70-page biography.

4. On the theatre context

Ernst Josef Aufricht: *Erzähle damit du dein Recht erweist.* Propyläen-Verlag, West Berlin, 1966. Recollections of the impresario who first put on *The Threepenny Opera, Happy End* and *Mahagonny*, in Berlin.
Denis Bablet: *Revolutions in Stage Design of the Twentieth Century.* Leon Amicel, Paris and New York, 1977.
Bertolt Brecht and others (eds.): *Theaterarbeit.* VVV Dresdner Verlag, Dresden, 1952. Account of the first six productions of the Berliner Ensemble, with drawings by Neher for *Puntila, The Tutor* etc., and stage photographs.
Hans Curjel: *Experiment Krolloper, 1927–1931.* Edited by Eigel Kruttge. Prestel-Verlag, Munich, 1975. Informative and well-illustrated history of Klemperer's opera.

Werner Mittenzwei: *Das Zürcher Schauspielhaus 1933–1945*. Henschel-Verlag, East Berlin, 1979. Achievements of the Zurich company before Neher's arrival there.

Henning Rischbieter (ed.): *Bühne und bildende Kunst im XX. Jahrhundert*. Friedrich Verlag, Velber bei Hannover, 1966. Well-illustrated account of the work of leading European artists for the theatre.

Günther Rühle: *Theater für die Republik 1917–1933 Im Spiegel der Kritik*. S. Fischer, Frankfurt, 1967. Comprehensive anthology of contemporary criticism of productions of the Weimar theatre.

Theater in der Weimarer Republik. Kunstamt Kreuzberg and Institut für Theaterwissenschaft der Universität Köln, 1977. Collective catalogue covering politics and theatre of that period.

5. About Brecht and others

Bertolt Brecht: *The Messingkauf Dialogues*. Methuen, London, 1965. Important theoretical work, with some relevance to design. Written mostly around 1939–42, but with some items (like the 'Speech' on Neher – see p. ooo above) added in the 1950s.

Brecht on Theatre. The Development of an Aesthetic. Edited and translated by John Willett. Methuen, London and Hill and Wang, New York, 1965 etc. See pages oo above for items quoted from this collection of theoretical writings. Further material will be found in volumes 15–19 of Brecht's *Gesammelte Werke*, Suhrkamp, Frankfurt, 1967.

Arnolt Bronnen: *Tage mit Bertolt Brecht*. Kurt Desch Verlag, Munich, 1960. On Brecht and Neher before 1924.

Friedrich Dieckmann: *Karl von Appens Bühnenbilder am Berliner Ensemble*. Henschel, East Berlin, 1971. Designs and photographs relating to eighteen productions, mostly of works by Brecht. They include those of *The Threepenny Opera*, *Coriolanus* and the *Little Mahagonny*. Appen was Neher's gifted successor, and obeyed certain of his principles in his own way.

David Drew (ed.) *Über Kurt Weill* and Kurt Weill: *Ausgewählte Schriften*. Both Suhrkamp-Verlag, Frankfurt, 1975.

Erich Engel: *Schriften*. Henschel, East Berlin, for East German Academy.

Werner Frisch/K. W. Obermeier (eds.): *Brecht in Augsburg*. Aufbau-Verlag, East Berlin and Weimar, 1975. Semi-documentary symposium containing many references to Neher and his sister before 1924.

Kurt Palm: *Vom Boycott zur Anerkennung*. Brecht und Österreich. Locker Verlag, Vienna and Munich, 1983. Includes a chapter on the granting of Austrian citizenship to Brecht, with some references to Neher. (The author is *not* the Berlin costume designer.)

Ronald Sanders: *The Days Grow Short*. The Life and Music of Kurt Weill. Holt, Rinehart and Winston, New York, 1980.

Jürgen Schebera: *Kurt Weill*. Leben und Werk. VEB Deutscher Verlag für Musik, Leipzig, 1983.

Klaus Völker: *Brecht-Chronik*. Daten zu Leben und Werk. Hanser-Verlag, Munich, 1971. English-language version: *Brecht Chronicle*, Continuum Books, New York, 1976. An invaluable chronology.

John Willett: *Brecht in Context*. Methuen, London and New York, 1984. Contains a chapter on 'Brecht and the visual arts'.

There are further English-language references to Neher's work in Rudolf Bing's and John Christie's operatic recollections and in Peter Heyworth's *Otto Klemperer. His Life and Times* (Vol. 1, Cambridge University Press, 1983).

6. Books illustrated by Neher

Bertolt Brecht: *Leben Eduards des Zweiten von England*. Gustav Kiepenheuer-Verlag, Potsdam, 1924. With

Left: Portrait of Brecht for the appendix to Brecht's first book of poems 'Die Hauspostille'

Right: One of Neher's illustrations for the published text of *Life of Edward II* 1924.

cover and four reproductions of line and wash drawings.

Aufstieg und Fall der Stadt Mahagonny. In *Versuche 2*, Kiepenheuer, Potsdam, 1930. Eight reproductions of projections.

Die Mutter nach Gorki. In *Versuche 7*. Kiepenheuer, Potsdam, 1932. Three reproductions of stage sketches.

Gottfried von Einem: *Der Zerrissene* Skizzenbuch. Wahn-Presse, Cologne 1964. Twelve drawings.

Lion Feuchtwanger: *PEP. J. L. Wetcheek's Amerikanisches Liederbuch*. Kiepenheuer, Potsdam, 1928. Cover and illustrations.

Hermann Kasack: *Aus dem chinesischen Bilderbuch*. Suhrkamp-Verlag, Frankfurt, 1955.

7. Articles on Neher in English

Mary Watkins Cushing: 'Caspar Neher'. In *Opera News* vol. 23, no. 16. 16 February 1959, pp. 13 and 29.

Martin Esslin: Caspar Neher. In *The Observer*, London, 8 July 1962.

Siegfried Melchinger: 'Neher and Brecht'. In *The Drama Review*, New York, Winter 1968, pp. 134–145.

Leopold Schreiber: 'Caspar Neher'. In *Gebrauchsgrafik*, Berlin, March 1934, pp. 2–11. Illustrated article with English translation.

For articles in German see the bibliography in the Von Einem/Melchinger book under 3 above.

List of exhibitions

1933 MUNICH Theatre Museum. Spring. (No details known).

1953 KIEL Kunsthalle, Neue Universität. A portfolio of Neher's drawings was shown.

1957 LEVERKUSEN. Organised by Rolf Badenhausen and the Bayer Works for CN's sixtieth birthday.

1960 COLOGNE Wallraf-Richartz Museum. April 2 to May 22. Subsequently shown at the Academy in Vienna (where CN was teaching). Catalogue: *Caspar Neher. Zeugnisse seiner Zeitgenossen*. Collection of essays with 37 reproductions.

1963 DARMSTADT Hessisches Landesmuseum. April 5 to June 4. (CN's work with Brecht). Catalogue: *Bertholt Brecht–Caspar Neher*. Ed. H. Regaller and H-J. Weitz. With 25 reproductions.

1964 AUGSBURG Schaezlerpalais (city art gallery). July 11 to September 6. Catalogue: *Caspar Neher Ausstellung*. With CN texts and curriculum vitae. Wahn-Presse, Cologne nr.6.

1965 SALZBURG Residenz-Galerie. June 20 to September 30. (Re CN's work for the Festival). Catalogue: *Caspar Neher und Salzburg*.

In the English-speaking countries CN's work appears only to have been shown (in small and unrepresentative numbers) at Covent Garden and the Metropolitan Opera. There was correspondence about exhibition projects at the Museum of Modern Art New York (April 1950), Sarah Lawrence College (April 1959), Columbia University's Brander Matthews Drama Museum and the Lowe Gallery at the University of Miami, Florida; but none of these are known to have materialised.

No exhibitions in other countries are recorded.

Sources and acknowledgements

Augsburg: Schaezlerpalais, Graphische Sammlung 42, 80, 88, 116.
Berlin: Berliner Ensemble photo Berlau, 67b; photo Paukschta, 11, 57b, 62b; photographer unspecified 134.
  Bertolt Brecht Archive 103a, 104b (both from film by Carl Koch).
  Brecht collection 6, 8b, 24b, 30a, 47, 50b, 55a, 58a, 58b, 60a, 60b, 64a, 64b, 96a, 96b, 103b, 104a.
Cologne: University Theatre Museum, Schloss Wahn 36, 53b, 78b, 83a, 83b, 86, 100b.
Darmstadt: Landesarchiv 19b, 90a, 90b.
Frankfurt: Film Museum 94a, 94b, 95.
Karlsruhe: Hainer Hill 5, 133b.
London: author's collection 137a, 137b.
Paris: Boris Kochno 24a.
Vienna: Austrian National Library, Theatre Collection 8a, 19a, 30b, 38, 40, 46a, 46b, 49a, 49b, 50a, 52a, 52b, 53a, 55b, 57a, 62a, 67a, 78a, 82, 85, 100a, 103c, 110a, 110b, 133a.
Zurich: Schauspielhaus 91.

Brecht's plays referred to in the exhibition and in this book:

Collected Plays

Vol. 1   Baal; Drums in the Night; In the Jungle of Cities; The Life of Edward
(*hardback* II of England; A Respectable Wedding; The Beggar; Driving Out a
only)   Devil; Lux in Tenebris; The Catch
Vol. 1i   Baal (*paperback only*)
Vol. 1ii   A Respectable Wedding and other one-act plays (*paperback only*)
Vol. 1iii   Drums in the Night (*paperback only*)
Vol. 1iv   In the Jungle of Cities (*paperback only*)
Vol. 2i   Man equals Man; The Elephants Calf
Vol. 2ii   The Threepenny Opera
Vol. 2iii   The Rise and Fall of the City of Mahogonny; The Seven Deadly Sins
Vol. 3ii   The Baden-Baden Cantata; The Flight over the Ocean; He Who Said Yes; He Who Said No; The Measures Taken
Vol. 4i   The Mother; The Exception and the Rule; The Horatti and the Curiatii
Vol. 4ii   Round Heads and Pointed Heads
Vol. 4iii   Fear and Misery of the Third Reich; Señora Carrar's Rifles
Vol. 5i   Life of Galileo
Vol. 5ii   Mother Courage and her Children
Vol. 5iii   The Trial of Lucullus; Dansen; What's the Price of Iron?
Vol. 6i   The Good Person of Szechwan
Vol. 6ii   The Resistible Rise of Arturo Ui
Vol. 6iii   Mr. Puntila and his Man Matti
Vol. 7   The Visions of Simone Machard; Schweyk in the Second World War; The Caucasian Chalk Circle; The Duchess of Malfi
Vol. 8i   The Days of the Commune
Vol. 8ii   Turandot; Report from Herrenburg
Vol. 8iii   Downfall of the Egoist Johann Fatzer; The Life of Confucius; The Breadshop; The Salzburg Dance of Death

Prose
Brecht on Theatre

ALSO
Happy End (by Brecht, Weill and Lane)

The following plays are also available (in paperback only) in unannotated editions:
The Caucasian Chalk Circle; The Days of the Commune; The Good Person of Szechwan; The Life of Galileo; The Measures Taken and other Lehrstücke; The Messingkauf Dialogues; Mr. Puntila and his man Matti; The Mother; Saint Joan of the Stockyards